Getting It Right the
First Time

Allyson

Best Wishes with
a Getting It Right."

6/7/13

Getting It Right the First Time

How Innovative Companies
Anticipate Demand

John Katsaros and Peter Christy

Westport, Connecticut
London

Library of Congress has cataloged the hardcover edition as follows:

Katsaros, John.
   Getting it right the first time : how innovative companies anticipate demand /
John Katsaros and Peter Christy.
        p. cm.
   Includes bibliographical references and index.
   ISBN 0–275–98479–6
   1. Business forecasting. 2. Business planning. 3. New products–Management.
   I. Christy, Peter.   II. Title.
   HB3730.K35 2005
   658.4'0355–dc22   2004022505

British Library Cataloging in Publication Data is available.

Library of Congress Catalog Card Number: 2004022505
ISBN: 978-0-313-35154-9

First published in 2005

Praeger Publishers, 88 Post Road West, Westport, CT 06881
An imprint of Greenwood Publishing Group, Inc.
www.praeger.com

Printed in the United States of America

The paper used in this book complies with the
Permanent Paper Standard issued by the National
Information Standards Organization (Z39.48–1984).

10 9 8 7 6 5 4 3 2

Contents

Preface

One of the benefits of working in Silicon Valley is the somewhat regular ritual of cleaning out your desk when you are moving on to a new job. There is nothing close to job security in the high-tech world, and you end up getting real good at starting over. If my dear father, who worked for one company his entire life, had lived to see his son change jobs more often than he changed cars, he would have been appalled. Today the following story seems closer to the truth: someone looking for a new job after twenty years with a prestigious computer company is told, "I like your background but I don't understand why you'd work for those guys for so long. There most be something wrong with you."

About twenty-five years ago, while cleaning out my desk when leaving one of my first marketing jobs, I clearly remember finding a sales lead listing from one of the early trade shows that we had attended to introduce a new product. I was struck by the fact that stuck in among a couple of hundred names on that list were names of people that I was quite familiar with because they eventually became our customers. In fact, most of our biggest customers' names were on that list. At the time I thought it interesting, but odd. If only we knew then what we knew now, selling directly to the names on this list would have saved us years of marketing time and lots of advertising money.

A few years later, while I was once again cleaning out my desk from a sales assignment the same thing happened. I found a list of names from an early trade show and—you guessed it—scattered throughout this list were the names of our most important customers. And, of course, the same thoughts crossed through my mind—what if we had just zeroed right into this list instead of scattering our marketing and sales efforts across a much wider universe only to find that our core constituency was right here in front of us all the time?

As they say, some things come in threes. The third time this happened I was in a company that was in a somewhat different position. Our company was nearly out of money. Before I had arrived there, the company had gone through several rounds of venture capital funding to develop its core technology without ever figuring out just what its product should be. With barely enough money to keep our engineering team together for a year, and after having disappointed investors through several funding rounds, we needed a new idea—fast. Instead of building the next great thing and seeing who would buy it (something the company had tried and failed to do already), why not put the process in reverse and find out what the heck it was that the initial group of people expressing interest in our core technology wanted in the first place. It was not so much about listening to what customers wanted since we did not have any real customers anyway and the technology that we were working on was only half-baked. I set out to crawl through a set of discussions with an eclectic group of individuals representing ultimate customers, other vendors, competitors, researchers—anyone who had expressed an interest in the technology—to find some common threads that would allow a company like ours to weave into a product idea. The results were fantastic in that we were able to find ourselves, our product, and ultimately our market. The really good news is that the company succeeded in launching a product that was a big success and eventually took the company public. The really bad news is that due to investor impatience, the ultimate beneficiaries of our success would be others. Nevertheless, I took away an understanding of something that is a sort of missing link in high tech—the ability to use research to improve and refine a business strategy.

It was not long after I left that last experience that I started the company that eventually became known as the Internet Research Group. Although it took several years to figure out what I was trying to do, what we eventually came up with was a business that combined market and technology research with strategic business planning. It took the better part of ten years to find out that a process I had been using to do research, something that we now call Expert Interviews, was, in fact, a potent process for exploring market opportunities that had not yet developed. Expert Interviews are a blend of sales and marketing because it uses a sales process—a situational analysis type discussion—to develop an overall picture of an incubating opportunity and a marketing process—profiling and categorizing clusters of business opportunities—to understand the strategic possibilities.

Although most of the high-tech world ignores it, market research is a huge business. If you worked at Pepsi, you would never think of introducing a new product without having lots of good focus-group session evidence confirming your strategies. If you are running a political campaign, you spend hours researching polling data before you finalize your media buy. If you are bringing a major motion picture to market, you gather lots of research including audience exit surveys from "sneak previews" as you develop your strategic plan. If you are managing a mutual fund, again, research is key to helping improve your odds. Research is not only a big business—it is a *fundamental* part the strategic planning process.

Why is it then that, in our world of high tech, research is dismissed as being irrelevant or that it barely exists at all? It is not because of lack of money. Entrepreneurs proposing new business opportunities to venture capitalists are asking for tens of millions of dollars in start-up funding. If they really wanted to spend some money on research in support of the development of their business plan they would only have to say something like, "Hey, Conrad (or Blair or whatever), I know that you're writing us a check for $25M but I need a little more because I actually want to do a little research to help improve my business strategy, is that OK?" The answer would, of course, be "Sure, go right ahead." The ultimate affect on the dilution of their founding stock would be inconsequential, but the ultimate affect on the value of that business would be extraordinary.

The simple answer that we have for why high-tech companies do not do much research in parallel with their strategic planning is that there is a long tradition in high tech of the "engineer turned entrepreneur"—the guy with a vision who figures it all out on his own. That might have been true for Bill Hewlett and Dave Packard who were starting their company in the days when Nixon was running for president talking about his "silent majority" (AKA unpolled masses). But the world has changed since then. Clinton would not have become president had he not figured what the polling data was saying. Likewise, the potential for success in high-tech ventures in today's markets can be vastly influenced by market input.

This research problem in the high-tech world is not just due to these problems on the demand side. The supply side of research is not so hot either. Out of the Gartner Group and the seven dwarfs, pick your favorite and then go back and read what they were writing during the early days of the Internet boom—that is, if you can find anything. The leading high-tech market research companies *completely missed* the Internet. Only after Netscape went public and the Internet was well covered by the *Wall Street Journal* and the financial press did any serious coverage of the Internet occur by the big research companies. (When Jupiter bought our company, the Internet Research Group, they were a third owned by The Gartner Group, and the strong rumor at the time was that Gartner's original investment in Jupiter was because Gartner did not want to be bothered having to deal with the Internet.) In our newsletter, we like to refer to these researchers as "those English majors from Connecticut" because of the fact that they have essentially turned into journalists focusing more on the entertainment value of what they are doing while forgetting completely that the role of research is to improve business strategy. As anybody in the political polling business will tell you, the answers are not in the numbers but in how you apply what you have learned to the problem of getting elected.

So, the problem with high-tech research is that it is broken both on the supply side and the demand side. Any MBA will tell you that if the customers are asking for the wrong thing, then it is not going to take much time for the supply side to start delivering just what the customers want, albeit the wrong thing. I cannot tell you how many times I have had CEOs tell me, "John, I can't afford to spend any money on research now but, don't worry, once we're successful, I'll buy all that I can." That is completely upside down. This attitude ends up wasting time and money as the company is forced to learn what they need to know "in the field." They should be saying, "I can't afford *not* to do research now." It is not about the money—it is about getting it right—the first time.

What we are attempting to accomplish with this book is to build the case for doing research up front in the planning process and to integrate research into the strategic planning process We also introduce a new research technique, "Expert Interviews," as a peer instrument to polling, surveys, and focus groups that is uniquely suited for high-tech companies bringing exciting new innovative products to the market. We hope you will both find the subject useful and the book enjoyable.

My wife, Robin, has been an inspirational part of the journey that has led to this book, and I am thankful for her patience and support while it all sorted itself out.

John Katsaros

When I first started working with John in late 1997, I was already heading in the right direction. My early background had been as a technologist (operating system designer and programmer), but I was always drawn to the adjacent topics of strategy or long-term direction. Over the years I had done pieces of that for Digital Equipment, HP, Sun, and Apple as well as helping found a computer start-up (Mas-Par). For the immediate years before joining John, I ran MicroDesign Resources (MDR), at the time certainly the leading boutique research firm specializing in microprocessors. I learned a lot from MDR's brilliant founder Michael Slater about the interesting territory where technical insight crossed business opportunity. Michael had built a strong franchise around those issues and the rapidly evolving world of microprocessors and Intel-watching. It had been hard to extend the MDR business into many other areas of semiconductors because they could not match the lucre of microprocessors. Michael had always thought that there might be analogous issues with the Internet. He turned out to be exactly right.

John and I have spent the last seven years immersed in the intersection between applications and networks. The exploitation of the Internet has created the perfect business opportunity to drive innovation and investment. Most innovation requires understanding the challenges posed by the reality of networking. As with microprocessors, bright technologists with deep insights drives progress, but as with microprocessors, business success requires understanding markets.

This book is all about bridging technology and business—marketing. There are no simple solutions. The kinds of people who create brilliant technical invention are fundamentally unlikely to see the market issues clearly. There are some renaissance "bilingual" individuals, but they are few and far between. Conversely, most brilliant marketers do not have nearly enough grasp of how technology evolves to drive fundamental direction. Brilliant business success requires a partnership. This book frames that partnership and shows how marketing and business analysis can be done early, in parallel with and as a contributor to early product development.

Having spent many years on the technical side of the coin, I am continuously amazed at the value of external insight. It is too easy to lock a team in a conference room and think that is the right way to solve a problem. If the answer depends on understanding the market, there is no substitute for talking to the market. We certainly cannot claim to have invented this concept; it is a fundamental tenet of marketing. Our innovation comes in *how* you do this, where the answer just is not clear. Surveys and focus groups work well when the right answer is understood by many and you do not have to think a lot about who to talk to, but that is never true for really interesting questions. Our fundamental insight is that for essentially all future market questions there is a set of experts who do know the answer. Using these methodologies you can find them, you can ask them the right questions, and you will get the right answers. I am regularly amazed at how well this works.

We live in a very complex and rapidly changing world, and there does not seem to be much likelihood of that changing anytime soon. But complex questions usually yield relatively simple answers when you find the right framework: "follow the money" is that kind of clarifying insight. At some level engineers love complexity; it is something they are very good at. If you are not sure what the right answer is precisely, add some more bells and whistles so you cover all the bases, and then let the market decide what the right answer is. It is a much better business idea to rotate the problem until it is clear what really counts, and then to focus on solving that problem well. This book is about how to do that.

My wife, Heidi Mason—a noted marketing and entrepreneurial strategist in her own right—has been an important part of my marketing education. As the "Car Talk" guys point out, there is nothing like a good dope slap at the right moment!

Peter Christy

Acknowledgments

This book has been a long time in coming, but we think it is the better for it. There was always more to say and we were always striving to say it in the best way we could. We hope our readers will profit from the extra time we took.

When we first met our editor, Nick Philipson, we thought we were just a few months away from completing this book. That was four years ago. If not for his insights and encouragement, we would probably still be stuck in the draft stage. We do not think we would have been able to go through this process of writing this book without his extensive help and generous support. So Nick is the one to thank if you find the book useful. Blame us if it is not.

We owe Martin Grossman our gratitude for reworking the manuscript. His help was invaluable. And we are indebted to our working group of twenty story reviewers for giving us candid readings of our understanding and ideas: John Anthony, Paul Bach, Sally Barlow-Perez, Steve Cox, Jesse Farnsworth, Evangeline Hutton, Tom Hutton, Joel Jewitt, Robin Katsaros, Dean Katsaros, Ron Kopec, Scott Landman, George Lao, Howard Lee, Milt McColl, Joanne McKinney, Andy Paul, Andy Preston, Maureen Richards, and Jim Willenborg. Each of them of them made contributions that strengthened the book. We are indebted to them all. And we owe a special thanks to our friend and co-conspirator Joanne McKinney for her help in assembling the listing of recommended Web sites which we have shamelessly added to our reference listings.

We have done our best to summarize what we have learned in our more than thirty years each in working with innovative companies.

There are lessons we have learned from having been in Silicon Valley through the heady days of Internet Gold Rush, and because we were deeply involved in the business of innovation both before and after that near decade of excitement, we think we have much to share that will be helpful to those who continue to innovate in its wake.

John Katsaros and Peter Christy

Chapter 1

Face Off: Skating to Where the Puck Will Be

Wayne Gretzky had it right: "I skate to where the puck is going to be, not where it is." He was talking about playing hockey, but sports have always provided good metaphors for discussing business strategies.

Anticipating the future is *the single most important thing* that a management team needs to do to succeed. Would your business life not improve dramatically if you could peek at tomorrow's *Wall Street Journal* today? Who could not make more money if they knew what the future had in store?

Seeing tomorrow's *Wall Street Journal* even a day in advance would make you brilliant at picking stocks. But sadly no one knows for sure what is going to happen, and that uncertainty can lead to a business advantage for those with better insight into the future. The better you can anticipate the future the greater your advantage.

In our work we regularly get to see how well people anticipate the future. As industry analysts we straddle both sides of business innovation: the sellers' side—bright people inventing, developing, and marketing leading-edge products and services—and the demand side—customers who gain business value through the early use of innovative products. Fortunately for us, unlike doctors and lawyers, there are no minimum requirements necessary to become an industry analyst, other than to have a reasonably professional looking business card. Vendors explain their view of the future to us daily in the strange ritual called an "analyst briefing," where companies trot out their senior executives to bedazzle us with their latest offerings and visions so that we, as known experts and pundits, in turn, will somehow "bless" them, thereby substantiating their view for less expert individuals, all the time hoping that the press will pick up on the enthusiasm and start writing glowing articles. In turn, this is expected to provide meaningful comfort and hope to those who might buy their product or service. Analyst briefings are to the innovation community what movie critic preview junkets are for the entertainment business—an important part of creating "buzz" around a product—except, unfortunately, we do not get the food, wine, travel, luxurious hotel suites, free massages, and gift bags that movie critics do. We are fascinated by the frequency with which companies show us plans that have only one chance in millions of succeeding. This is like having a young boy show us the drawing of the Pokemon robot that he wants so badly to build and that must have special powers, remote control, and work perfectly under water—a compelling vision but one that we, as adults, know will never happen. These companies have all the creativity and enthusiasm of seven-year-olds, and unfortunately this often blinds them to their business plan's shortcomings.

When a company's executive team comes to tell us about the exciting business they are building, there are just three things that we really want to know from them (and that we think they should want to know as well): (1) How big is the market (and how fast is it growing)? (2) How different are they from their competition, and how long do they expect any key differences to last? and (3) How does their business model capitalize on this market opportunity?

There is a condition that we call "no-fault marketing" that has been raging through our industry like an out-of-control fire. It happens when marketers take it for granted that a market exists for any new product their company develops or *why would we have built it in the first place*? No-fault marketers do not let facts like market size and growth get in their way. They burn money and resources without plan or purpose. And since they have not taken a position on what it takes to succeed in the first place, when things fail it is no fault of their own. They are never wrong. We have learned not to take anything we are told at face value and have grown somewhat cynical in the process. We have found that the best thing to do is to remain skeptical, find out what the underlying market facts are, and then interpret these on our own.

By the time a company briefs us they are about to culminate lots of work and introduce their offering with great fanfare and hoopla. They have spent millions of dollars on development, the products are in early adopters' hands, and the big launch at a gala affair is just a few weeks away. But when we ask them the most basic and fundamental questions—who is going to buy it and why, how big the market is and in what segments, how are they different, how does their business model work to their advantage, how they intend to win against their equally bright, energetic and well-funded competitors—the discussion degenerates quickly. The company tells us about the handful of eager early customers they have found, and how pleased they are. We in turn, recall for them the old TV ads for an over-the-counter drug that told us that "three New York doctors recommend Miracle Medicine!" The impact of the drug claim fades rapidly if and when consumers realize that you can find three New York doctors to recommend just about anything. In the same way, we believe that an innovative idea can garner a handful of interested customers—say three chief executive officers (CEOs), whose companies are all too often funded by the same investors as the new product's inventor, rather than three New York doctors. But with a multimillion-dollar investment it is not OK to just get a handful of customers. You have to tap into a rich vein of customer demand that can lead to big market opportunities, growth, profit, and, ultimately, a handsome return to investors. A few eager customers are no substitute for evidence that a substantial market is just around the corner.

Sometimes we can be sympathetic because the executives are dazed survivors of the dot-com investment boom, where you did not have to create a real business. You were given tens of millions of investment dollars just to create buzz and momentum that led quickly to a public stock offering with huge gains for the both employees and investors. But that Camelot has long since faded, and we're back to the "good old days' when real revenue and profits matter—you have to build companies the old-fashioned way, by finding customers and getting them to buy product. There are still a few of the surviving-but-not-public companies from the dot-com fantasy era around, now in a hopeless position, having taken down an obscene amount of investment when the money was easy, that have the proverbial chance of a snowball in Hell of ever producing a commensurate return. They might as well owe a bookie $50,000 and try to pay him off by working at McDonalds flipping burgers.

Unfortunately it is not just the dot-com survivors that present impossible plans. Many come from newly funded companies and sometimes from innovative teams at larger companies—groups that should be able to answer our simple questions. All too often, they do not have any answers. They seem unable—or unwilling—to anticipate market changes.

Are the days of producing significant ROI on investments in innovative products and services gone forever? Should innovators just give up on trying to build important and exciting new businesses? Nothing could be further from the truth. Just follow the money. You need only to look at the magnitude of current venture investment to see that plenty of capital remains to support innovative ideas. But we certainly do believe that too few of these ventures make an effort to anticipate markets far enough in advance. To take advantage of the extremely profitable opportunities that inevitably appear in every era, innovative companies must look ahead. They must anticipate.

THE RETURN FROM GETTING IT RIGHT THE FIRST TIME

Anticipating demand is the best way to make certain an innovative company (whether it is a start-up or an established company with the will to reinvent itself) can achieve breakthrough success. To take full advantage of the rewards of anticipating a market, the trick is to *get it right the first time.* Too many companies only get it right by the expensive and painful process of trial-and-error. They finish the product and *then* take a year to learn about their markets by exploratory marketing and selling. After those experiments, they focus their resources on what worked. What if they did more anticipation of the future while the product was being developed and as a result found the high yield markets twelve months earlier? What kind of a difference would that make? Here's what we think:

1. First of all, it is really expensive to do learning when you are all staffed up with sales and marketing. When a product is launched, the company is burning cash at the greatest rate by far in the company's young life. That additional year will cost a lot of cash, often half again as much as what they have spent up to that point. If the company has to go back to its venture backers during that period for more money, it will cost the proverbial pound of flesh and could easily dilute the employees' equity position by a third.

2. When the product is announced, the competition will understand what the company is doing and, during that year, have time to make their moves in the space, thereby diminishing the market available to our company. This can cause another one-third erosion of the downstream valuation due to lower sales volume caused by competitive erosion and competitive pressures on price.

3. And then there is the opportunity cost The twelve months spent searching for the right solution might have been used for other company efforts such as planning for and prototyping the next product. This might cause it to miss a chance to add perhaps another one-third to the valuation.

4. Bringing the company to success a year earlier not only means a greater return but also an earlier return, therefore, faster liquidity. Given the time value of money, that is really important to the investors.

So according to our crude, back-of-the-envelope estimate, the company that gets it right the first time can yield as much as a 400 percent return on the original investment; the company that takes a year to find its way will yield only a 66 percent return. The actual result probably will be that the return to investors is even higher for the company that gets it right while the returns to the other investors are probably lower.

How well does this work in the real world? Here is one particularly vivid example. A small U.S./U.K.-based software company named Striva got it right the first time. Founded in 1999, Striva provided enterprise software for change data capture (CDC) and real-time and bulk data movement from mainframe systems. Although all the "action" had moved away from mainframes, Striva's management team recognized that more than 90 percent of large enterprises still used mainframes as part of their mission-critical information flow. Further, Striva saw that for enterprises to get a real-time view of business health via their operational information warehouses, they would need to upgrade their systems using the types of technologies that Striva was building so they could extract data quickly from mainframe systems (rather than using the traditional overnight extraction batch processes).

Despite the recession and the conventional wisdom, Striva built out its mainframe software products and marketed them as important additions to corporate information warehouses, mostly using joint marketing agreements with the industry leaders to keep down their marketing and sales expenses. In 2003, the information warehouse leader Informatica was being threatened as Oracle started to build out its data warehousing capabilities. As part of its plan to stay ahead of the competition, Informatica gobbled up Striva for $62 million. Not a bad outcome for a four-year-old software company with less than one hundred employees.

Striva produced one of the best venture capital (VC) returns in 2003 in terms of both the amount of money returned to investors and the speed with which it was returned. The second round investors saw their return in less than a year! And all because Striva got it right the first time.

THE ROLE OF DISRUPTION

Anticipating the future is a major problem for innovative companies because traditional methods of market research are not effective at predicting the disruptive changes that high-tech innovation brings. In his best-selling book, *The Innovator's Dilemma,* Clayton Christensen cites this as Principal #3 of disruptive technology: Markets that do not exist cannot be analyzed. That is a very important statement, because what he is telling innovators is that the most important thing they should be looking for is a *disruptive* opportunity and then turning around to note, by the way, that you cannot analyze its impact because the market does not yet exist. Although we completely concur about the potential importance of disruptive change, we differ in that we believe those future markets can be analyzed. Christensen is absolutely right that you cannot analyze markets that do not exist—*using traditional methods of market research and analysis.* But that is because traditional tools—focus groups, quantitative studies, surveys, and the like—were all developed to study markets that do exist. If you are running a research business, there is much more money in researching things that do exist than things that do not, so not surprisingly that is where the research tool and methodology efforts have gone first. Our point is simple—you can indeed understand markets that do not yet exist *if* you are willing to use some new methods and are willing to go patiently through the process of looking "under the radar" for evidence of the elements needed to ignite a market.

To be fair, high technology market strategy was never a very well-developed art. In earlier high-tech years, strategy was not so important. Markets were small, and products were exceedingly innovative. There were fewer competitors. Time was less of a factor. The technology spoke for itself and it was often all right to bring an innovative product out and discover the market after the fact. Companies such as Oracle, Cisco Systems, Network Appliance, and EMC have similar stories of evangelizing their technologies for years before they were adopted by mainstream buyers.

During the dot-com boom, whatever market anticipation practices had existed previously quickly disappeared. What is the point of trying to understand market growth and competition when your mission in life is to go public in a frenzy of irrational enthusiasm? Another nail in the marketing strategy coffin was that during the dot-com rage purchasing was remarkably "horizontal." Everyone was getting the same Internet stuff—GM was no different from GE or from Pfizer. It did not make much difference what business you were in, everyone needed to move frantically to the Web so they did not get "Amazoned" by a newly funded competitor. If everyone is buying the same stuff, it is a waste of time to worry about what their business is or how the technology contributes to their success. Who needs strategic marketing?

Whether it is because the principals never really believed in strategic marketing or stopped doing it during the dot-com boom, most of the companies that we see tell us (in other words) that they did not do any real market anticipation. They have done nothing much to characterize future demand for their ideas, instead preferring to pick what seems to be the best market approach and to run it up the flagpole and to see who salutes. As one CEO proudly told us, "I'm a believer in jumping into the pool and *then* learning how to swim." This type of thinking—market strategy development via sequential experiment—is unfortunately the norm for high-tech companies who would never do something so crude as part of their technical product development. The simplest reason that few people make the effort to better understand the future is simply that they have never seen it done and something they are not going to figure out how to do by themselves. If trial-by-fire strategy development was good enough for companies they worked for previously, why change it now? If you want a competitive advantage—better still, an *unfair* advantage—then it is time to turn on your market headlights to get better idea of what is coming down the road. This book will show you how.

People who have never done market anticipation do not know where to start or where to go. If you do not know what you are looking for, predicting the future is indeed a daunting task because the future gets big quickly. It is impossible to figure out the future of everything going on in business, but it is very possible to figure out the immediate future of what is happening in the areas that matter most to you. That is our secret!

MARKETROCITY

It does not take subtlety to show where a little anticipation would have made a big difference. We spoke earlier of business plans with no hope of success. There have even been entire industries that suffered dearly for their collective refusal to rationally consider the future. Our favorite is probably optical data networking.

During the great optical networking boom of the late 1990s, there were over 700 independent companies funded, each requiring at least $50 million to bring a product to market and grab a chunk of the new optical networking landscape. In retrospect, this was a completely hopeless overinvesting, but during the heyday, these companies would come by to brief us on what they were doing. Invariably they would share with us wonderful forecasts in which they got a small chunk of a huge and rapidly growing optical data communications market. If they could just grab a modest share of this new, exploding market, their future would be assured, and they and their backers would become fabulously wealthy.

These presentations came off the track when we asked our nasty little questions about the market—where's the beef? Understanding data communications is in a sense no more difficult than understanding the economy. The key insight that you have to gain about the economy is that it all builds on the needs and purchases of individuals. Just as an economy is built from the bottom up, one person at a time based on what they consume, so is data communications. Somehow the huge data volumes that were required to fuel these forecasts had to derive directly from what individuals were going to do. Please explain to us, we asked, where all this data will come from. Where will the demand for so much data traffic come from and how does it grow? And if you do not mind, start with scenarios about real people like you and me.

The problem was that those companies (and the industry as a whole) could not come close to doing that. We got dead silence. How could we have our heads buried so deeply in the sand not to understand the potentiality of optical data networking? So we would next point out that it seemed to us that there is a limit to how much communications infrastructure an individual (and therefore a population) could consume. We reasoned that a private digital high-definition (HD) TV channel for each man, woman, and child in country—the pets had to share—was a reasoned maximum consumption (in technical terms that is around 20 million bits of data per second). From our experience, an individual with a compelling, personalized video channel is unlikely to do anything else; their senses will be fully engaged. So what happened, we asked, if that was all there was? Unfortunately for those 700 optical data companies, the total data needs of even this market just did not add up to what was required to make all the companies operating in this market wealthy. It was not that fiber optics was bad technology, rather it was too good. When you can send hundreds of billions of bits per second over a single optical fiber, you just do not need many fibers—or lasers or high-speed routers—to make it all work. The technology and the basic ideas were fabulous, but the market anticipation was fatally weak. Too bad for all of those 700 companies and their backers.

It turns out that none of those companies (even the big networking companies like Nortel or Juniper), had ever asked those simple questions, and needless to say, they really did not like our simplistic, back-of-the-envelope calculations. One of the visiting CEOs literally started to explain that we had left out the communications required for the refrigerator to talk to the grocery store, prompting us to ask whether they were exchanging "need more milk" requests—which requires very little data to be communicated—or home movies of refrigerator construction in the factory—which produced meaningful amounts of data but obviously did not make sense. One CEO became visibly upset when he realized, a little too late, that these are completely reasonable questions and that someone should have asked them a long time before. Since the era of those rather entertaining briefings, the optical data communications market crashed just as hard as or harder than anything in the dot-com space did. We do not claim that the lack of demand was the only failing (there were many), but it is a sufficient line of questioning to have predicted accurately the collective disaster by itself.

The point of this story is simple—these companies were not being driven by demand but instead were operating in a false economy, one fueled by irrational exuberance and overinvestment, just as the dot com bubble was. The investment rate in these companies surged without regard to demand. Demand for networking capacity shot up slightly because of the arrival of the Internet boom, but it certainly was not surging to the levels necessary to support all of the optical networking companies that were forming. And because these products were so much better and had many orders of magnitude more capacity than what they replaced, ultimately demand was more than satisfied with a tiny amount of the new stuff. The world was much better off for the introduction of all the new optical data technology. And in the end, the consumer got the benefit more quickly because of the foolish investments that were made without sufficient market forecasting! But it did not change the world in the way the emerging optical networking companies had hoped for and needed in order to justify the investments. Most of these companies were put out of their misery as soon as the financial markets realized how much these companies had overbuilt capacity.

WHAT'S THE ALTERNATIVE?

If you are seeking high gain and leveraging some form of disruption there is no excuse whatsoever for evading the task of understanding your market and the demand it will reasonably create. Whether or not you have ever done this kind of market anticipation, we are here to tell you that you really can do it. Our methodology is ultimately based on a skill that we can safely predict almost all readers of this book have: the ability to have a meaningful discussion with a subject matter expert in an area of high mutual importance—to use our terms, to hold an "Expert Interview." No matter what you are trying to do, if it is going to be anything like the next big thing, then there are important precursors well under way now, and there are hundreds of smart people engaged in those activities in all sorts of roles. If you can be clear about what you need to know (your little piece of the future), you can find scores of those individuals who will be more than happy to discuss their passion with you, and those discussions will tell you more about your future than you can imagine possible today.

Expert Interviews are as straightforward as they sound—interviews with people who know much more than you do about a particular subject. For some reason, researchers often turn up their collective noses when it comes to chatting it up with experts. We have been brought up in the business world to believe that there is a certain mystique to the research process and that the only good research must have statistical blessings and high price tags. Expert Interviews break away from traditional research by putting you at the scene of potentially disruptive industry events, which is exactly where we think you should be. We often use the time-honored detective series *Colombo* to help illustrate what we try to accomplish with Expert Interviews. As soon as Colombo arrived at a crime scene, he would begin looking for clues. He considered everything important—cigarette butts, shoelaces, how knots were tied. Colombo would collect all of the evidence that he could and then start to form an opinion of how the crime occurred and who the perpetrator was. Similarly, Expert Interviews provide the clues that can help you see what is likely to happen.

We will show you how to combine Expert Interviews with a decision-oriented methodology that lets you anticipate what customers will be doing in the near-term future. Then you can use this information to help you sell more of your product or service by identifying top customers and key market segments in advance of entering the market, strategically positioning your company in the eyes of its prospective adopters and catching the developing disruptive trends that are about to surprise your competitors. As you will learn, accurately anticipating the future is not that difficult to do. By doing this, you will make better decisions and you will avoid the completely off-the-mark assumptions that permeate and ultimately destroy whole industries—as the optical communications industry was destroyed. By using the right strategy and the right tactics, you have a good chance of *getting it right the first time*.

Chapter 2

Anticipating Change:
The Case for Savvy Planning

Observe always that everything is the result of a change, and get used to thinking that there is nothing Nature loves so well.
—Aurelius Antoninus

Men in Black

Chuck Schwab once said that the worst day of his life was when he sold his company, and the best day was when he bought it back. You do not get the full meaning of that until you have experienced it firsthand. We learned about where conventional market research works and does not work by selling our company to a conventional firm, becoming conventional market researchers for a while, after which we went back to our old methods and had a much better understanding of why it was so much better.

In our former lives, along with our other partners, we sold our research and consulting company, The Internet Research Group, to Jupiter Communications. Jupiter had recently gone public, setting a new valuation model for research that we liked, so we had built a business plan that said we were going to do the same thing. Jupiter had jump-started their success with an investment from Gartner, and we went out to get money to do the same. Jupiter seemed like a good prospective investor for us, as Gartner had been for them. But they wanted to buy us and not fund us. Since that is what we had wanted to do in the first place, it was OK with us.

As part of their investment in Jupiter, Gartner had helped Jupiter understand their successful model of research, and Jupiter adopted it (or adapted it in their Silicon Alley, SOHO Manhattan existence), and as part of Jupiter, we got to learn it, too.

Our principal belief is that it is important to know as much as possible about the markets that you were trying to serve, although that comes at a considerable cost in time and focused effort. "Just the facts, ma'm" as Joe Friday would say. Jupiter knew better. They did not depend on knowledgeable industry veterans as analysts—they hired smart and articulate people, it just did not matter if their recent degree from NYU was in comparative literature. What did matter was that they looked and acted cool—shaved heads and expensive black T-shirts were ideal. A short-lived CBS sitcom *Welcome to New York* captured the style perfectly with the line "We don't wear brown, Jim, we wear black till something darker comes along."

Our real-world, eye-opening experience continued as we realized that Jupiter did not do the kind of research we had been doing. Our goal was always to make direct contact with selected senior thought leaders and decision-makers. Jupiter was happy to farm out e-mail or Web surveys to whatever list their subcontractors used. What counted was getting questions answered, not so much whose answers you were counting. The Jupiter methodology was great for the dot-com frenzy period when all you wanted to do was get a piece of the action, whether or not the action made any sense. Having bright boys and girls in black commenting on broad surveys from unknown users captured the state of the herd, and gave a name to the trends, but it did not help anyone really understand what was going to happen.

The problem with their methodology, of course, was that it was a system guaranteed to reflect the general consensus—it acted like a mirror reflecting the prevailing wisdom. The way you find out what is going to happen is to ask intelligent questions of carefully selected knowledgeable individuals, and for that shaved heads and black T-shirts are more of a hindrance than a benefit.

In the end, Jupiter was a perhaps ironically a victim of its own methodology. When we showed up it was pretty evident that Jupiter needed to enter new markets if they were to continue to grow. Soon thereafter, as the bubble began to burst, the issue of new markets became even more urgent. As marketing experts, we knew what to do. If you need new markets, you can go out and find out what people want and how they buy it, and if you have something to offer, craft a product to enter the market. That is what marketing is all about and what market research is really useful for. But in 2000, as the roof started to fall in, the boys in black had no time for that discussion. Market research—not to mention market strategy—was something for their customers but not for them.

They did not listen. We left and restarted using our original business model, richer and wiser for the experience, painful as it had been. We returned to our research methodology, knowing a lot more about why it was the right thing to do.

CHANGING TIMES

The business of innovation has changed. Great new inventions alone do not have the staying power they once did. The speed with which competitors can replicate new ideas and continue to garner investment capital quickly means that getting it right, right away and right now, is more important than ever. A recent example is the market for software designed to block e-mail spam. In 2003, this emerging category had more than seventy-five competing vendors with over $150 million of venture funding pursuing a $180 million market. In 2004, investors continued to invest even more in new anti-spam companies, despite the expectation of most experts that the market will ultimately be able to sustain only a handful of players.

In addition to the availability of capital to fund new product development, the speed with which customers can deploy new products and services has made the environment radically different than it was just a few short years ago. Customers once had many obstacles to hurdle whenever they added infrastructure. This naturally slowed the pace of technology adoption. Adding new functionality was not a simple process and often involved building network extensions, making physical changes, deploying new user equipment, and training. Now that has all changed.

Most industries have reached a sort of technology parity where industry leaders have matched one another's competitive advantage and are vigilantly looking for new ideas that can improve their businesses. Consequently, the value propositions are more modest than they were ten years ago when companies could gain substantial long-term differentiation. These more modest value propositions mean that innovative companies have no alternative but to get things right on their first try—there is no longer time to make mistakes in *this* market. Market mistakes may result in an innovator with a great new idea creating a fantastic new category only to see competitors quickly swoop down and capture the market's sweet spot.

Mini-Bubble

Spam is also a great example of how rapidly today's markets can emerge and how rapidly companies must respond if they are to capture the opportunity and produce significant investor returns. Spam, as we all know, is unwanted e-mail. Before 2003, spam was a niche problem, and only a handful of companies offered products that addressed it. One start-up named Brightmail would come by every once in a while to update us on their progress. They agreed that spam then was still a small problem, but they argued that it was growing more alarming by the month as spammers became more sophisticated. They kept focusing on this one number—spam growth—realizing that if it kept up it would be the key to their eventual success. Brightmail's approach to spam control was centralized; they used lots of "honeypot" mail accounts to look for and categorize new forms of spam, so they had a remarkable view on what was flowing through the network and how it was growing. Spamming is basically a numbers game. It costs essentially nothing to send spam (the underlying problem), so the more volume you can blast out to e-mail accounts the better your potential returns. As spammers became more sophisticated in the volume distribution and subtle masking of spam their methods got very affective at distributing huge volumes of e-mail. The impact of spam changed dramatically when spam volumes finally began to exceed 50 percent of the traffic sent on the network. When the percentage of spam was less than 50 percent, most mail system operators and administrators thought of spam as a "user" problem, which mail recipients needed to sort out by themselves. When spam percentages exceeded half of all e-mail being sent, that all changed abruptly and e-mail operational costs were dictated by the spam traffic; increasing spam volumes required more servers and storage and increased the network costs of mail. Suddenly, controlling the flood of spam was anything but an end-user problem. In less than a year, anti-spam solutions went from being exotic pattern-matching technology for particularly sensitive end-users to critical operational software needed by every company running an e-mail system and every service provider operating a consumer e-mail service. In other words, everyone needed it.

Maybe more vendors could have and should have anticipated this abrupt change in buying behavior, but most did not. Brightmail was ready. In the blink of an eye, a mini-bubble appeared. Customers needed something quickly, and it was a sellers' market. Investors were looking under any rock for an anti-spam company to fund. Suppose you had a company that responded to change with the traditional eighteen-month product cycle? Or what if you were a high-tech investor but had not been paying attention to this corner of the market and needed to investigate it? By the time you respond you have lost the opportunity in a hot market and are hopelessly behind. The same time frame that was generous to you in the past no longer exists. Today's markets are fluid—opportunities are fluid—you have to be able to respond immediately to unexpected changes and opportunities. Brightmail had been looking ahead and was in the right position to move quickly. They became the market share leader in an increasingly attractive anti-spam market. Then, with a remarkably clear sense of timing, Brightmail filed for an initial public offering and then, before completing the offering, sold itself to Symantec, itself a hot and rapidly growing security software provider, for over $370M. By the end of 2004, Brightmail was one of the few spam bubble companies that produced a significant return to its investors. At the time of the Brightmail acquisition, valuations (as measured in the comparison of market capitalization to sales revenues) for anti-spam vendors were astronomical. It was a new niche bubble. They are not likely to stay high. Going into 2005, there were more than seventy-five companies in the anti-spam business beating up on each another for meaningful market share with nervous investors biting their fingernails, hoping that they will see an attractive return before the bubble bursts. We are cynical enough to believe that all of this spam technology is self-defeating to the spam investment proposition because the control systems will put spam back in the box (or can) as an annoying problem but not a critical one. We are pretty sure that the customers will realize that before most of these doomed investors do. Part of getting it right is getting the investment timing right too.

The "Internet bubble" marked the peak of innovation's overinvestment phase. During that time, the glut of investment capital—ranging from venture investment to technology capital spending by large organizations—drove the cost of capital toward zero and flooded companies with business opportunities. The impact was not just limited to a bunch of kids running dot-com companies; as cyber start-ups went public, it caused significant concern in companies like General Motors and Merrill Lynch, which were worried about getting left behind by dot-com startups whose bright futures and fabulously high market capitalizations made Blue Chip companies nervous that their futures were in jeopardy. Even media giants like Time-Warner got nervous as evidenced by its disastrous merger with AOL. During the "field of dreams" phase, innovative businesses adopted a "build it, and they will come" approach to any idea that seemed to have merit. The prevailing wisdom was: "Why waste the time with market analysis and planning?" Instead, the mantra of the moment became "Build it! Promote it! Monetize it!"

Following March of 2000, when the dot-com bubble burst and the steep downturn in the high-tech economy began, excitement about innovative new products and services rapidly declined. Even seemingly solid high-tech companies found their marketing departments ill equipped to cope. Companies just kept right on chugging along until they got hammered in ways that had seemed inconceivable in better times.

It is clear to us that businesses producing innovative products and services will face a much different market environment in the decade to come. In the past, innovators had the luxury of simultaneously serving customers in many diverse market segments with high value propositions placed on their innovative solutions. Due in large part to the massive build out of the infrastructure that was occurring, and to the great value that these investments could yield, businesses and consumers spent lavishly on getting wired. New project investments—as measured in either total dollars spent or number of projects funded—were at an all-time high. Never before had so much VC money been tossed at so many start-up ventures with such abandon. But that has changed. Unfortunately or not, for a long time to come, spending on innovation will not be as broad based, nor will value propositions be as uniformly high.

Customers Are Pretty Savvy

Today's customers are much more aware of the value and uses of innovative products and services than they were even a decade ago. In the "old days," innovative companies were selling into "greenfield" situations—whether it was a consumer buying his first Fax machine or a huge company installing an enterprise customer relationship management system, the story was similar—customers went from having nothing at all to having a complex piece of technology. In the 1980s and 1990s, most customers of innovative products were essentially first-time buyers, and sellers were in a position where they could define their companies around the product that they made. Vendors like IBM used terms like "systems companies" to talk about the fact that they provided complex systems, implying that customers needed the value-added "smarts" that only a systems company could provide. That has all changed. Today's customers are well-seasoned technology buyers. They have been spending lots of money on technology for more than a generation. Consumers, small business operators, large enterprises, governments, and education customers all have experiences with buying innovative products and services. They are not dumb and probably know a lot more about the stuff that they are buying than many of the people selling it to them. Now, the systems company is the customer, not the vendor. Today's vendors must *fit in* and *stand out* within the context of the systems that the customer operates.

Companies selling innovative products and services need to align themselves to these new market realities; most successful innovations will serve fewer market segments with, hopefully, a more complete offering providing great value. Most businesses have reached technology equilibrium, and further business gains will come from market-specific differentiation. Potential customers will be looking to understand how innovative products can make them more competitive within their industry.

The business of innovation works best when customers are willing to pay a premium to acquire the product or service. For the innovator, that is much more achievable when they are selling to business customers that are both profitable and expanding. After all, a profitable and growing business is expanding—which means they care about things like winning new customers, keeping existing customers, business improvement, employee hiring and retention, and improving relations with business partners and customers. Companies that are either flat or shrinking have fewer of these issues and are often saddled with unused investments from past projects. When companies shrink, they are shedding resources. The value propositions that innovators are likely to provide to customers that are not growing and not profitable are greatly diminished. Consequently, these value propositions will be much less likely to generate price premiums.

Between 2001 and 2004, Merrill Lynch reduced its workforce by 24,000, closed more than 300 offices, retreated from several international markets, and eliminated several lines of financial services business. During that period of retrenchment, it was hard to imagine Merrill Lynch placing much hope on innovative new technologies to help its business. Its markets were collapsing. Gaining market share was not the issue. And as far as cost savings are concerned, having implemented its widespread workforce reductions, Merrill had already taken its most potent cost savings initiatives. In that situation, it was not realistic that innovative new technologies would yield much in the way of substantial business improvement. Yet by 2004, after Merrill had restored itself to health and started looking to gain share in important markets, it would naturally be receptive to more aggressive business improvement ideas.

The fact that in most major business sectors companies have reached technology parity is shifting many value propositions from business improvement to utility operations. In a bank, for instance, a large portion of the technology budget keeps its automatic teller machine (ATM) network functioning. ATMs were once a potent force, significantly shifting market share and restructuring customer relations. But today, the ATM wars are mostly over, and operating an ATM network at a bank is similar to operating a power utility—keeping the system operating is job one. These shifting value propositions, from business improvement to utility computing, have real consequences for the way in which innovative new products and services need to express themselves in the market.

Innovative companies now have no choice but to adopt new strategies in response to changing market circumstances. The impact of shortened development cycles, abundance of investment capital, and the wired economy as it exists today have all conspired to wreak havoc on traditional planning techniques and the research processes that were built to support planning. Today's executives need to anticipate future market conditions correctly to succeed, and to do that they will need to develop their ability to look out in time further than their next development cycle. Hitting the mark right the first time is just as important for digital watch manufacturers like Casio as it is for software development companies like Microsoft or for jeans manufacturers like Levis. In most industries in today's economy, the time from idea development to volume manufacturing has shrunk. The complete life cycle of a modern digital watch takes less than a year from concept to design to high-volume manufacturing. So the hot watches that will be selling by Christmas are barely through the conceptual stage the January before. Similarly, Levis has less than a year to develop and put into volume production new fashion products for one of its key market segments, teenage girls.

There is no longer time for "experimenting in the field." The months and years that it takes to figure things out can result in missing the mark completely. Innovators pay a stiff price for not getting it right the first time. In the future, market conditions will only continue to shorten design times and take more time out of the system. The price of waiting will only continue to grow.

Not too long ago Kyocera acquired the cell phone division of Qualcomm and turned a troubled product line into a success. Qualcomm, long an innovator in cell phone technology, had trouble with establishing a market for its handsets. The key to success came when Kyocera turned the division that had introduced one new product a year into a group that produced a new product each month. More product introductions meant that rather than producing a general purpose product, they could instead target specific markets with separate products. This greatly reduced the time it took to put new ideas into the hands of their customers. When you can bring twelve new products into the market each year, your marketing department can target specific customer segments and does not have to anticipate the market as far into the future as does the group that only infrequently changes its product line.

Compared to just ten years ago, time has compressed. Business moves much faster today then it did a decade ago. This feeling that time is compressing will continue as business continues to move even faster. Many of the new innovations on the horizon hold the promise to squeeze even more value out of existing business processes and further shrink time to market. Unfortunately, however, most companies seem to have given up on the process of anticipating future demand, choosing instead to learn about their markets in a trial-by-fire manner as they always have. As macho as passing through the fire sounds for learning about markets after product introductions, companies are taking enormous risks by doing so. Today's markets change so quickly and are so unforgiving, there generally is no time to make substantial business modifications and to still be the market leader. Instead, innovators must anticipate market preferences in order to get it right the first time or risk not only their ability to dominate a market but even to survive.

For innovators, success in today's economy, when it comes, will rarely be broad based across many market sectors simultaneously. This is the type of oversimplification that often gets us into trouble. Naturally, there is no business law that governs this, and there will be plenty of exceptions. But we think that the reality of the next ten years is that companies building innovative products will be faced with having to deal with a future of succeeding across a handful of market segments.

Perhaps the biggest implication of this is that these companies will have to expand their product offerings—in other words they should probably plan to do more for fewer customers. This, in turn, means that funding for future innovation will adjust to these future realities. Since the potential returns may be more modest, the funding levels required to produce a positive investment return will eventually align to these new realities (meaning, of course, that innovators will have to get the most out of their resources). The fact that market opportunities in the future will be more modest may be less of a concern for big companies such as IBM and Microsoft than for venture-backed start-ups, because the bigger companies are in a better position to expand their value by incorporating greater functionality to supply more of the complete systems they provide. IBM's recovery in the late 1990s was built from one big idea—focus on the customer solution as the unifying concept for their broad product offerings.

Thanks in large part to the huge amounts of venture capital available to innovators with reasonable business plans, the business of innovation has been expanded. Innovators are no longer just garage shop start-ups or skunk-work projects in larger corporations. Investors are studying every new product category, looking for their "next big thing." Researchers comb through markets trying to find hot spots of customer demand. And there is plenty of funding available, so even bad ideas get plenty of money. The payback from one success will be much greater than the losses from nine failures. The competition for new ideas—from start-ups and big companies alike—shows no signs of letting up.

Another big difference in today's innovation markets is the speed at which new products can be brought to market. Development cycles that might have once taken three to four years have shortened to twelve to eighteen months.

The availability of venture capital and the speed at which new products come to market means that if you have a new idea that attracts a lot of customer attention, you are guaranteed that you will quickly have a multitude of competitors—both from start-up companies working in a similar area and from much larger competitors looking to extend their product lines.

THE CHASM IS CLOSED

During the dot-com insanity, everything happened at breakneck speed. Part of that was in response to the hype and a willing suspension of disbelief, but characteristics of the build out of Internet infrastructure for both consumers and businesses have made the pace of technology deployment fundamentally faster (which in turn makes it imperative for marketing to move more or less in real time as well). In the days of the mainframe, and later in the client/server computing era, putting a new application online would take years because so much "stuff" (things like constructing proprietary networks to deploying specific desktop software to working out the standards issues for transferring information) was needed before the application could operate. That caused the chasm effect, where innovative new products had built-in market delays that significantly postponed sales while customers built the essential infrastructure components needed in advance. But today these chasms have closed. The infrastructure is built, the standards are agreed on and are implemented, and networking is ubiquitous. There are fewer delays in the innovator's pipeline. Consumers and business customers are much more adept at putting innovative products to work.

It Didn't Used to Be Like This

One of this book's coauthors worked at Digital Equipment during their heyday and has a lot of fond memories including the birth and growth of DECNet and the VAX computer line. DEC was a great example of how you could be disdainful of marketing and still succeed. The head of DEC Engineering distrusted marketing, warning internally of the evils that were sure to follow if MBAs were hired. To be fair, DEC succeeded by being quite attentive to the market, albeit after the fact. Ken Olsen's idea was to let great engineers build great products more or less for themselves, see what the market did with them, and then respond with agility.

The VAX-11/780 and VMS, the operating system software that drove the VAX, were great examples of the process. The products were designed and built by DEC's best engineers using an engineer's perspective. The driving force behind the VAX was the fact that memory was getting cheaper, and the economically "right" amount of memory for DEC's minicomputer product line did not easily fit on 16-bit computers. That drove the imperative for 32-bit minicomputers, and with that motivation, DEC went ahead to build a damned good 32-bit computer and operating system.

The marketing plan was another matter entirely. The VAX-11/780 product marketing plan theorized that the VAX market would divide neatly between "real-time" and "transaction processing" applications. This was not surprising since it was more or less what the PDP-11, the VAX's 16-bit predecessor, was used for. Of course, what happened was very different and much more exciting—DEC's VAX created the departmental computer: something that could do more or less what a mainframe did but with a price and usability suitable outside the glasshouse. Fortunately, DEC did not take its own internal marketing group that seriously and happily went with the market flow as it appeared.

The reason that DEC could afford to misinterpret the market and still succeed was that when all of this happened, twenty-five years ago, the business world was very different. Innovative companies had more time and fewer competitors than today. If your original marketing plan did not work, there was time to retrench and figure out what to do. Marketing groups that failed to "get it" would eventually be told by the sales force what customers were doing with new products and what they needed in the way of new features. DEC did not invent departmental computing (their customers did), and left to its own devices, DEC's marketing group would have missed that train completely. But back then the market was forgiving, and this gave DEC the time it needed to reinvent its marketing plan around what customers told them to do.

The world moves a lot faster now because of the existence of standard infrastructure of the sort provided by the Internet. Back in the good old days before you could innovate the application you had to lay miles and miles of infrastructure, which took years to complete. Now you just use the infrastructure in place. The world is less forgiving now because the action is at the application level and not the operating system level. Left to themselves, engineers will argue for years about the right editor or the right way to design virtual memory. End users just want to get a problem solved. DEC's distrust of marketing (and no shortage of other quirks) started to inflict considerable penalties, which led to its painful public decline and culminated in an ultimately even more painful acquisition by Compaq. Better marketing might have changed the outcome. It is still possible to see the continuing DEC marketing legacy (especially in Boston-area start-ups)— management that happily takes the products engineering creates and drops them into the market, after which they search for the right way to sell it. You could do that in the 1978 minicomputer market, but in case anyone missed it, that was a quarter century ago, and the idea is now, shall we say, considerably past its prime.

You often hear marketers describe this sort of situation— retrenching from an initial launch—as having fallen into the chasm. "Chasimists" like to say that it takes time for a market to develop, time during which the early adopters can experiment with a product and provide feedback that vendors use to develop additions and extensions in the product line to make it more appealing to the broader early majority. And back then, they were probably right. Customers who wanted to use innovative new ideas like distributed computing needed lots of time to get to where they were headed. That is not the case anymore. Today's innovative businesses have to enter the market at the right point right away. Like a basketball player on a fast break, you take a shot; if you miss, you lose the advantage and give the defense time to rally.

Infrastructure requirements have always been one of the not-so-hidden "gotcha's" in the world of information systems. A new client server application had the promise of really improving the business, but it first required that a client/server infrastructure be put in place, which likely as not required an upgrade of PC desktops to a common and more current operating system, the construction of a new network (or consolidation and bridging of existing networks) to connect those desktops to the servers, and finally the installation and operation of a new set of second tier servers to build the multi-tier client/server architecture. All of that needed development with careful piloting, and the net of it all was that you had to be really good to bring a new application into use in less than a couple of years. Not only did you have to get everything in place before the application was brought online, but running the application meant keeping the entire infrastructure in place and up to date, not a trivial matter.

The Internet and the Web substantially change this. The network part (standard protocols and general interconnection) means that users can be connected to servers immediately—no "laying of track" is needed. Every modern PC comes with a browser, so we do not need any special client software either anymore. On the server side, the Internet created an important new category of Web server—systems especially created to deal with Web access—eliminating still more annoying details in the construction of a server-based application.

The biggest acceleration benefit is server-based, network-accessed, applications. The Internet means that all the users who must collaborate for a given business process (e.g., supply chain management) can share a common application. This being the case, a fix or functional improvement to the application impacts all users immediately. Previously a new version of an application would be developed and then staged out to the various groups of users, which could add months (or more) to the product evolution process.

Internet Time—It Really Is Faster

During the dot-com insanity, everything happened at breakneck speed. Part of that was hype, but some characteristics of the Internet do make the pace of Information Technology (IT) development fundamentally faster in today's markets than ever before. Compared to the previous era, two factors are fundamentally different: (1) the Internet infrastructure is already in place and (2) the rapid deployment of incremental server based functionality. Before these factors combined, you had to be really good to bring a new application into use in less than a couple of years. Not only did you have to get everything in place before the application was launched, but running the application meant keeping the stuff in place and up to date—not a trivial matter. Today powerful applications can come online much more rapidly than their predecessors, and evolve much more rapidly as well. All of that puts a much higher premium on getting things more or less right from the beginning rather than muddling through, comfortably limited by the natural evolution timescale of the infrastructure.

Internet time also impacts business decision making. Only a few years ago, any business that wanted its customers to interact with its computers needed to build out its own proprietary network to do this—the metaphoric equivalent of putting up your own ATM network to provide the direct user interface. In addition, the computer networks at the time were mostly built on proprietary structures, which might have been good for a few applications but did not provide a broad platform that other applications and systems could share. Today, of course, that is not the case. Business and consumers come prewired. And because they are already online, Internet time is compressed even more.

Network-based applications can come online much more rapidly than their predecessors; they evolve much more rapidly as well. All of that puts a much higher premium on getting this more or less right from the beginning rather than muddling toward the truth, comfortably limited by the natural evolutionary timescale of the infrastructure.

The consequence of this new innovator reality means that now, more than ever, as we need to emphasize again and again, your business strategy has to be right at the outset. Companies no longer have the time to make mistakes in the market while letting valuable months slip away hoping an idea will find its customer base in the market. Innovation has become a sophisticated business with little tolerance for mistakes. If you have an opportunity window, it might only be open for a year. Losing even a month of this opportunity can be a major setback. The whole idea of getting it right the first time is to let you find the open windows in the market and climb through them before they close. What is essential to the innovative company is to develop a business sense equal to the engineering savvy it has to build a hot new product. Put the two together and you have an entrepreneurial organization that is primed to succeed.

Chapter 3

Looking at the Future

You can observe a lot by watching.

—Yogi Berra

Anticipating the future is a major problem for companies involved with innovation, since traditional methods of predicting the future do not work. The reason that new innovative markets are not well understood using traditional research alternatives is really simple economics. Big agencies and research companies cannot afford to be experts on pre-emergent markets because there is little money in it. If the market has not yet formed, then there are not enough big clients interested enough to provide a market for the research. Market research for emerging markets is an oxymoron. Like jumbo shrimp, market research on disruptive technology is a contradiction in terms. Predicting the future, of course, turns out to be a really big problem if you are involved with innovation, since traditional methods of figuring out the future do not work all that well. In fact (as noted in chapter 1), in his best-selling book *The Innovator's Dilemma*, Clayton Christensen cites this as Principal #3 of disruptive technology: "Markets that Don't Exist Can't Be Analyzed." So if these markets cannot be analyzed and if there is not enough money to support syndicated research, the common wisdom is to do nothing. That is precisely what happens when companies wait until their first products are ready before they go out to test the market.

Although Christensen makes a good point, we think that it might be better to say that markets that do not exist *cannot be analyzed with traditional techniques*. That, of course, is because traditional techniques were not designed to make sense of emerging markets. In disruptive cases the past no longer predicts the future, but that does not mean the future is unknowable. When you begin organizing input from people who are experts in the business that you are looking into, then you will start to see where your pucks may be going. The idea is obvious in a sense: You do not ask the sportswriters what play to run; you ask the best coaches and players. By the time the sportswriter knows, it is too late. And of course, once the sportswriter knows, then everyone else knows too. If you wait for a new business opportunity to appear in the *Wall Street Journal,* you have missed your chance. The future is discernable, if not obvious. Early on, however, only a few facts are evident, and they are only visible to a very select set of individuals. These are the people who have struggled the longest with the challenges at hand, have some progress to report, and can relate their experiences.

FOLLOW THE MONEY

Every successful salesman has an effective scheme for qualifying prospects—validating that someone has the means and authority to buy the product you are trying to sell. There is no law against a twelve-year-old boy wandering around a Ferrari showroom, but the chances are he will not buy. There are interesting exceptions to the rule. In the late 1960s, Grace Slick, the lead singer of the psychedelic rock band Jefferson Airplane, walked into the San Francisco Ferrari dealership with the goal of buying one. A snooty salesperson intercepted her and informed her that "these cars cost a lot of money, I'm afraid." She pulled out a paper bag of cash, handed it to him, and smiled saying, "Is this is enough?" These days, when it comes to high-tech products there are many fewer Grace Slicks, and from what we can tell, too few marketers understand how to qualify customers and markets.

As a result of what has transpired in the economy—huge boom followed by huge bust—the market validation process has broken down. Instead of following the money by understanding the depth and breadth of market opportunities, during the boom economy people got in the mode of following the idea. Not too long ago, a couple of bright guys with a clever idea could sketch it on a napkin during a lunch at Il Fornaio in Palo Alto, have $20 million in funding by sundown, and be off writing code that evening. Later on, a friend from an earlier venture would be invited to head marketing for a few months. The designated marketer (DM) would start the process of market validation by approaching a couple of customers he knew and telling them, "I'm working with Jim and John [legendary visionaries]. Would you like to hear about our new product offering?" The answer would usually be yes. (Given that it was such a simple question, how could you say no?) The DM would check the first box for "market validation" (why else would they want to hear about it—clearly it is an important product). The discussion would occur, feedback would be solicited, and the "customer" would probably say, "Boy that's an interesting idea!"— meaning if somebody actually gave these guys money it would be stupid to insult them, and they probably know a lot more about this than I do—and the DM would check the second box for "market validation." A few months later the product would be ready for beta testing, the same customer would be approached, and they would ask him if he were interested in being a beta user. The answer was often yes (meaning, "why not, it won't cost anything and boy will my friends think I'm cool and maybe they'll let me in on the friends and family stock when they go public"), and the DM would check the final box and close the issue of market validation.

What is the flaw in all of this? No one ever asked whether there were enough customers who would spend enough real money for the solution. Talk is cheap but money speaks. DMs often have "happy ears" when they are talking to customers, choosing to recall only good comments and never really seeking critical commentary. Admittedly it is challenging at best to ask whether someone will spend money on a new product that is not working yet. Fortunately, there are some good ways of predicting the answer. Our secret method is this: Get experts in the industry to tell us what kinds of problems we could solve with this new product, even if we needed to tweak it a bit. Then find out how much money is already being spent to fix problems like this and what the business advantages are that can result—how does this new widget give its customers an unfair competitive advantage? It is possible that a company is going to change how they spend money based on some cool new product, but if you think of it in terms of solving business problems and gaining competitive advantage you can get a pretty good understanding of how much it is worth. The critical step that our DM missed was that he never asked the customer whether they had a real business problem that they would spend real money to solve. Or, to put it another way, he did not follow the money.

Pedal to the Metal

A few years ago, when the Linux open source operating system was virtually unknown in the business world, Hewlett Packard wanted to revamp its UNIX product strategy. At the time, Sun, IBM, and HP were beating the daylights out of each other competing for market share, each company having customized their own variant of UNIX, packed with proprietary features targeted at software developers and workstation users. The UNIX market had matured to the point that most big customers had picked a vendor and were unlikely to switch. After discussions with roughly one hundred experts working at the cutting edge of this market, it became clear to us that the fastest growing and largely underserved portion of the UNIX market was for special purpose functional servers used in datacenters—things like e-mail servers—where they would be set up to provide a specific function and then run with little change or intervention. The proprietary high-touch features that the big-three vendors had built into their UNIX versions were not needed by this new market and in many cases were an inconvenience. What the customers actually cared most about was server density—how to get more performance into a smaller physical space—and the ability to tune the operating system for optimal "pedal to the metal" application performance. While these fixed, functional applications were a small piece of the multibillion dollar UNIX server market, they were growing at a much faster pace than the rest, and there was no incumbent to push aside. Many analysts thought that HP was crazy when it introduced its Linux server strategy because it would cannibalize its own highly differentiated product line. But in reality, HP was entering the fastest growing segment of the market, a segment that was wide open. The insiders—those experts who were at the center of a disruptive event—had the right answer one more time.

KNOWING WHAT YOU KNOW YOU DO NOT KNOW

When companies are telling us about their newest products and services, we usually ask a simple question: "How big is the market and how fast is it growing?" Quite often we are told something like,

"We're not really sure how big the market potential is, we'll just have to wait and see, but when it happens it will be really big."

That might sound like a reasonable answer, and it is probably truthful, but it seems to us that it is the wrong answer. It amazes us that companies spending millions on product development and investors putting tens of millions into these same companies appear not to have the slightest clue when asked to forecast market size. Maybe they do know and the market potential is so small that it is worthless, in which case their start-up is really a substitute for a grant-research project. Sure, there is a lot of guesswork involved, but at least they should take a stab at trying to figure out how and why demand will change over the next few years.

Why is this process broken? These companies are spending millions to develop and bring their products to market. They certainly have the money to find out what they do not know. But the problem is not just that these companies know so little about the market size. They also do not seem to know much about what customers value and why. This is a violation of the rules of Marketing 101, and it is sadly pervasive. Why do they pay so little attention to consumer wants and needs? Perhaps it is a matter of inexperience. It is a historical fact that, in the innovation universe, the focus has been so much on product engineering that too often the markets are ignored.

For whatever reasons, historical, temperamental, or otherwise, most innovative companies:

- do not anticipate demand,
- do not differentiate themselves,
- do not distinguish their value propositions, and
- do not understand the possible outcomes of their strategic initiatives.

Just as professional sports teams hire scouts and rely on scouting reports to get facts that they do not already know in order to prepare for a game, innovative companies must develop their own scouting equivalents to ensure success.

But what scouting techniques are right for innovative companies? Research is big business—estimated at more than $10 billion per year. And like any big business, research has migrated toward serving its customers. Among research's largest customers are consumer product companies and political candidates. Consequently, the tools of these researchers—focus groups, surveys, and polls—have become focused on those instruments that are most effective for these large research customers. These methods have been continually refined and have become sophisticated, scientific instruments for measuring consumer reaction. If you are running a consumer products company or running for office, these research tools are almost always necessary and can create an important fact base from which to plan your strategy. That is what they are designed to do. But if you are running an innovative new company, these research instruments do not help you much and, in fact, may do some harm.

Spam: Because We Care about Our Children

Often the hardest thing about being an industry analyst is staying awake—some of the company briefing sessions that we sit through are so mind-numbing that sleep seems a higher form of consciousness. Lately we have found that not laughing is running a close second as a vocational hazard. We were completing an in-depth research study on the subject of spam when the CEO of a company came in and told us that their reason for spending time in this market was to make sure that their children could grow up in a spam-free world. (Does anybody have a box of Kleenex?) As comedian Steve Martin would say, "Ex-cuuu-se me." Children have nothing to worry about on that front—at a time when there were over seventy-five companies bringing some sort of spam-blocking system to market, you would assume that at least one of these systems might actually work. Your children will not have to worry—at least not about spam. Yet when we asked the CEO how the business of selling anti-spam systems in a fast-moving highly competitive market was going to develop, all we got was a blank stare, followed by a metaphor that we hear a lot: "We're not really sure what's going to happen, we'll just jump into the pool and then learn how to swim." The danger with this thinking is, of course, that you run the risk of drowning before you have time to learn swimming fundamentals.

The enduring legacy of innovation is transformation—innovations transform business sectors. A rough rule of thumb is that the greater the degree of transformation, the greater the value that customers will place on the innovation and the more they will spend to acquire it. So if an innovation is really important, then it probably holds a lot of potential to transform something. And for anticipating the future, it may just be that the thing that is getting transformed is more important to study than the actual thing that does the transforming. While this may sound like the obvious thing to focus on, in the early days of a new technology it is often hard for the start-up team to separate "what the product does" from "what is the impact that it may have." Again, we find this classical marketing theory—find out what business you are in rather than simply what your product is. It is not rocket science, but it seems foreign to so many innovators that you might say it just does not compute. Plus, it is really hard to do. So, rather than trying to predict the future of a new product in a new class, it is simpler to look at the product's potential impact on what will be transformed in order to understand the value of the transformation and the speed with which customers will rush to acquire it. This focus on the impact of the transformation may be both simpler to understand and more revealing in terms of understanding an innovation's potential well in advance of its entry into the market.

It is not easy to anticipate where business is headed, especially in fast-changing markets. Over the past fifty years, research disciplines have emerged that help executives gain better insight into their customers' intentions. Research is an optimization game; a fractional spending in your marketing budget should provide enough leverage to generate significant profits. If you are a movie executive planning the release of a blockbuster, it makes all the sense in the world to spend money on focus groups to test the movie's trailers so that you can improve their effectiveness before spending millions on the launch. Dollar for dollar, that is money well spent.

Since we are in the research business, we often get feedback from management teams telling us that they are not interested, unable, or even unwilling to do *any* market research. One of the most perplexing reasons that we are given is, simply put, "we don't have the budget for it." Being strong advocates for research (hey, we have to get our kids through expensive private schools and on to college, and this gig is all we've got!), it is hard for us to comprehend this objection. Their company is probably spending millions on their development efforts in trying to bring a new product to market as fast as possible. They are usually either a venture-funded company or an internal group within a larger company, and their multimillion-dollar development effort is not yet a money maker. So the idea that somehow spending a relatively small amount of money on research is going to hurt their bottom line is preposterous. Yet, they can convince themselves that early on in the development cycle is not the right time to develop a clear vision regarding what market demand will look like just when their hot new product is ready to sell. Worse yet, they will tell us to come back later, after they are successful, telling us that they will have plenty to spend on research then.

This thinking is completely upside down. Market research needs to be done in parallel with product development. The earlier you do it the better. The idea of spending on research after you are successful can only mean that you have got such a big ego that you just love reading about yourself. You do not need it then. The products that most companies are working on have relatively short shelf lives. There are narrow windows during which companies must get the most out of their R&D investments and use their development budgets to build what is needed. Companies that wait until their products are almost finished run the risk of wasting months and months of time while they learn in real time. Spending on research earlier in the product development cycle will yield terrific paybacks, which can significantly improve a company's chances of making a market.

We think that traditional tools for listening to customers—polls, surveys, and focus groups—do not work well for innovative-driven companies because these instruments are designed to interpret mainstream thinking. For innovative areas, conventional wisdom does not matter. The traditional tools are designed to find where the majority opinion lies. Innovative companies do not care so much about the majority opinion since they are out to change the status quo.

The process that we use for determining the impact that highly innovative companies will have on their markets is something we call the "Expert Interview." The methodology that we have developed for organizing input from industry experts provides the vehicle for accurately predicting the future of fast-changing markets and for anticipating customer demand. It is important to consider the Expert Interview as a peer to traditional research processes and a method that is highly effective for collecting input in fast-changing markets situations. As relevant as focus groups are to the consumer products industry, Expert Interviews have the potential for unlocking the secrets of highly innovative market potential.

The biggest objections that we get to Expert Interviews center around the concerns that (1) there is little on which to claim statistical significance since we are not getting input from large numbers of people, and (2) the experts performing the research are encouraged to drive the discussion, be skeptics, and not to trust everything they are told. Our methodology runs counter to what everyone is taught regarding traditional polling and surveys. We have found that having comprehensive in-depth discussions with even just a few experts can reveal vast amounts of information about how market demand is likely to evolve. And for many emerging categories, there just are not a lot of experts available. So our answer to the objection about lack of statistical significance is: "If you want statistical significance, then go interview a large number of people who do not know anything about the subject and you will end up with a completely wrong answer but one that is, nevertheless, statistically significant." We also encourage the interviewer to be an active participant in the discussion and not go through a rigid questionnaire, which also raises concerns by traditional researchers. And our response to this concern is that experts have their own unique perspectives and knowledge base. They may be expert only on a portion of the subject matter. It is up to the interviewer to find out where the expert has relevant input.

For innovative companies, understanding the potential of their new products means that you have got to have a sense for what is going to happen in the future, and that means you will need to expand your knowledge beyond majority opinion. When you are trying to understand the future, the key issues are who you talk to and what questions you ask. Finding the right people is critical.

Think about the problem from a future perspective in which you have 20:20 hindsight. Suppose some interesting transition in your business has occurred, and *after the fact*, you are trying to understand it. In most cases, you could find a couple hundred people who were not surprised that the transition took place. They might even tell you why this transition was predictable. In other words, as a result of their experience or involvement, they *expected* the transitional event. For example, the Internet was around for twenty years before it became a household appliance. While no one could predict that the Internet was going to be the catalyst for the biggest business valuation increase in history, it was possible way back in 1993 after talking to experts with first-hand experience to predict that Internet technology was going to have far-reaching implications onto the future of information technology. Likewise, if you analyzed the potential of the Linux movement before the mass media popularized it, you might not have gotten the absolute growth rate right but you could see its ability to build out its initial important customer constituencies. The key to tracking each of these fast-moving disruptions was to put aside the popular concepts of what was important, find the experts who were doing important work in the early phases, and learn what they had to offer as their explanations about the potential impact their work would have. And then, by coupling their proposed visions of acceptance with a reasonable view of reality, you could judge for yourself whether these were areas that were important to you. These two examples have had, of course, larger impacts than most technology disruptions, but they do serve to make the point that important disruptions do not just happen overnight. There are significant developmental stages to the process, which involve people with special skills and an ability to try applying the underlying technology to a new situation—people that we call experts.

Now flip back to the present and envision something that you are interested in doing. It makes sense that again there are quite a few people out there who might help you understand the outcome; you just have to find them. These are the individuals we will be focusing on. They are the experts. They are the early adopters. They are the principals in the companies already active in the space. Together, before you even start down a new path, they can paint a remarkably accurate view of the future.

And then there is the parallel issue of what you ask those experts once you start talking to them. Polls and surveys use a restricted question set across all respondents. If you are talking to an expert, the last thing you would want to do is to restrict your question set. In fact, you would want to do just the opposite; you would want the ability to ask deeply probative questions to help develop your insight into how the world may be changing.

The best answers come from a relatively small number of very knowledgeable people. A big reason why we are not fans of broad surveys as useful for understanding innovation is that you will get answers to all of your questions, regardless of whether or not the respondents know what they are talking about. Why ask someone about something he or she does not have an informed opinion on? Or worse yet, why ask someone who might have the wrong answers? When it comes to new technologies that are not yet widely known, more often than not, the viewpoint of the majority is not relevant because the majority does not have enough familiarity with the technology to understand its potential. Or worse yet, the majority opinion tends to favor the status quo, feeling that things are good enough today and that changing things is not worth the effort. There is a famous tale of market research blundering that tells of Ford Motor Company surveying its markets, asking what customers wanted, and then building its biggest failure—the Edsel. Meanwhile, GM simultaneously surveyed the same market and asked not "What do you want in a car?" but "What does your neighbor want in a car?" and as a result modernized the Chevrolet, its biggest success. The story probably is not entirely accurate but the moral is: It is easy to get misled by surveys.

Furthermore, we also do not think focus groups work well as a technique for predicting the future for innovative products and services. Focus groups are good for getting qualitative information about how consumers might react in the short term but are not much use for getting insight you need to have from specialists. In-depth conversations with experts are all but impossible in a focus-group setting for a variety of reasons. If you find an expert who is willing to share some time with you, why dilute that input in a group session and subject it to the distortions of the group? If you find an expert, we think you should learn as much as you can from this expert and understand his or her perspective. Then repeat this again with other experts until you have assembled the information you need. For consumer marketing, surveys and focus groups are essential tools. But for long-term market anticipation, which is what businesses care about most, surveys and focus groups are inefficient: they take too long to set up, cost too much, and yield too little useful information. They also suffer from the fact that the process involved with surveys and focus groups ultimately ends up distancing management from actual customers.

What about giant surveys and statistically significant percentages? Naturally, research companies would like you to think that the only good analyses are those that they create, and that the more expensive they are, the better. And while there are a few situations where big budgets may be needed, the vast majority of situations involving highly innovative companies are those in which the company itself has become the leading expert in the area and will remain so until well after the innovation has taken hold. Furthermore, business executives have been trained to think that market research is some sort of mysterious process that is only good if it costs lots of money and is supported by industry research analysts working for large agencies and big research houses. Worst of all, there is the strong belief that this is something that you cannot or should not do yourself. Nothing could be further from the truth, and the results speak for themselves. Like many things in business, practice makes perfect. The results will not be perfect the first time that you anticipate how a market will develop. But after doing it a few times, your accuracy will improve.

There is another problem that you might have with believing that you can predict what is going to happen in your markets. In today's world, forecasting has come to lack credibility and is often ridiculed by the listener. If you heard someone on the radio say what the stock market would be like next year, you might listen, but you probably would not believe it. If you saw someone on TV making a prediction about the economy, you would be skeptical. Unfortunately, if someone comes into your office and says they know what will happen to market demand in a certain area, you lump this in with all the other forecasting charlatans. As a society, we have become immune to forecasts, either because they are generally unreliable or because they are being promoted by special interest groups. And of course, nowadays pundits have become all too commonplace in the news media. This further raises the noise level, making it harder to separate out fact from fiction. These days, entire cable network channels focus on forecasting business trends.

Most of us have learned, sometimes the hard way, what a complex world we now live in. Volatility—the rate at which business conditions change—is at an all-time high. Years ago, in an age where people often spent their entire working lives at the same company, management could create five-year plans and actually believe in them. Today, you would be laughed out of the boardroom for showing a five-year plan. Even the kid in the mailroom knows that the next thing on the board agenda might be a merger or acquisition. As a result, we have all but given up the idea of predicting what is going to happen.

We are not asking you to change this attitude. What we are pointing out is that while long-term macroeconomic planning might be extremely error prone, *a look at a shorter time frame can and will be accurate enough for successful business planning.*

So if you jettison surveys and focus groups, the two most basic techniques marketing groups use to get information, what do you do? Simple: find a few people that know a lot about the situation you are considering because they are actively involved in it and talk with them. These are the people who are at the scene of the crime with respect to your specific idea. The general name that we give this core group is "experts"—the people, who either due to choice or circumstances, are currently engaged in the subject to some extent. Our experts may have a deep knowledge of the situation or they may just have important experiences with one or two aspects of the problem. In other words, they hold a few pieces of the larger puzzle that we are trying to put together.

The Expert Interview breaks from traditional research practices in three main respects:

1. There is no randomness to the process of finding who you are trying to speak with—you actually search for the people that you are trying to talk to.
2. You do not use a research assistant with a prescribed set of questions—instead you use an expert like yourself to have a discussion with the experts that you are speaking with.
3. You do not accept all of the data that you are told—rather, you consider the areas that your expert knows the most about to be where the input you received is strongest, and then you decide on what is and is not relevant to your investigation.

And now, when it comes to those discussions, the real art comes in. Our method is to first find these people and then engage them in long discussions about what is happening now, and what is likely to happen, and why. How you talk to these experts is as important as finding them. With interesting people you need to have interesting discussions to glean their wisdom. The traditional research tools force a structured question set into the interview. First of all, you do not typically talk to experts just about specific product reactions or desires. Imagine what would happen if you happened to encounter a politician or celebrity at a cocktail party and started to sound like a pole taker? Instead you would want to try and understand what really lit their fire—what were they passionate about and why (that's the part you don't discover easily on the evening news). All the same applies to the use of experts in research. You are interested in a much bigger picture view. What do they do? What drives the concept from a business standpoint? What are the big challenges? How did he or she become an early user of these applications in the first place? Perhaps most important, how do they spend their money and why? With Expert Interviews, a structured question set actually stands in the way of you finding out what you would like to know. Instead, it is important to develop a conversation with the expert that first lets you determine where his experience and knowledge base is focused and then lets him teach you what he knows. You want your experts to guide you through the process so that you can understand their perspectives.

The next challenge for getting Expert Interviews done right comes in finding the experts whose insight you should seek. Who are they? Are they among your existing customers? Are they competitors? How about your competitors' customers? Are they complementary product providers? Are they the venture investors? Are they the industry analysts? Are they the technological gurus? Are they today's market leaders? Are they the young Turks in the start-up garage? The answer to all of these questions is yes, but we have not mentioned the key "experts" yet—the customers who can gain the most from this innovation.

The job of finding the right people to speak with gets more challenging and interesting when you have to answer the question, "Just exactly who are those early adopters?" Again, there is a simple answer: these are the people who have the problems that they feel are worth solving. The real difficulty comes when you try to combine these answers to figure out what to do. How do you start down this path? What are the first steps? Where are the road signs? That is why we have developed the Three-Step Anticipation Process:

1. selecting alternatives,
2. anticipating where they are going, and then
3. considering the factors for success.

It is a process that will help build the experience and knowledge you need to anticipate demand yourself. The process begins by understanding and organizing what it is that you already (and often uniquely) know. You might be surprised to find that you are the key source of ideas. Is that not what marketing "experts" are for? But the fact of the matter is that you almost certainly possess more useful information than you would ever imagine. This is the time to extract and organize it by listing the markets and potential applications that you have talked about in early product-planning discussions, in the search for beta customers, and as part of the investor due diligence process. That starts to build a set of potential alternatives based on these questions: What are the applications that are most like this—or likely to use this—new technology? In which market sectors is there the greatest interest? Who stands the most to gain and why? With some thoughtful effort and skill, you can hone in on what seem to be the most relevant applications.

Next you need to find the movers and shakers in those areas; for example, the customers who are most likely to give you clues to understand where the alternative may be going. For businesses, the most important input comes from the customer who can gain a significant business advantage. That is your number one expert, because if you solve that customer's problem, you can propel his or her business. So that customer is the expert on both the problem and the solution. You can give this customer whatever name you want—the innovation user, the early adopter of new technology or services, the people who have struggled with like problems, the people who have real experience. You need to find people currently involved with these situations, and no one person will have all the answers that you need. After gathering information from them all, you will mold the information into your own view of the overall situation to form your best guess scenario about where it might be going.

For example, if you wanted to understand the demand potential for an innovative new product that has the potential to completely disrupt the market, how would you go about doing it? One solution is to find market projections from a large research company. But because it is an innovative new category you are interested in, forecasts are not available, so you have to rely on existing research looking at the market that your plans will, essentially, disrupt. The conundrum, of course, is that what you are doing replaces not only the existing products in the category but also the existing market research. So you are left to use research and forecasts that, if you are successful, are wrong.

We are suggesting that you divide your world into possible opportunities (alternatives), convert your possible opportunities into outcome scenarios, figure out how much demand will change in the next twenty-four months (know where these opportunities are going), and thereby, determine the feasibility of converting your scenarios into realities and achieving your goals.

You have got to score goals to win in hockey. And scoring goals means getting to the puck. Since the goal is to win, scoring goals and taking good shots matter. But to take shots, you have got to get to the puck, which means that you have to figure out where the puck is going.

Chapter 4

Knowing Where and How to Move

*Research is simply to find out what you are going to do when you
can't keep on doing what you are doing now.*

—Charles Kettering

Hall of Shame

Many years ago the Boston Consulting Group used a quadrant
(a 2 × 2 graphical matrix) to depict different businesses depending
on profitability and growth. They created cute descriptive words
with cute pictures like "Cash Cows" and "Dogs," which have
endured as standards, and created a presentation standard where
the right place to be was clearly in the "upper right-hand corner."
The quadrant is a great visualization tool because it can present
complex concepts as a simple intuitively provocative picture.

It has come to a point where no marketing presentation is
complete unless, toward the end, there is a quadrant showing the
presenting company and their chosen competitors, and lo and
behold, the axes and metrics have been cleverly defined so that the
company is at the rightmost, top most point in the graphic. Voila,
they are the *winner*! During a week, we can have five different
companies come by, all in the same market, each showing us their
own version of a competitive quadrant, with each presenting
company in the upper right-hand corner in each case.

Two things bother us about this, and they should bother the
perpetrating marketers. First, overuse has rendered magic quadrant

descriptions meaningless. The dimensions—the axes and metrics used for comparison are generally what we call the "ilities"—you know, marketing buzz words like scalability, reliability, usability, maintainability—and do not reflect any basic customer sensibility or requirement. But what we find most worrisome is that despite these glaring problems, many of the vendors actually seem to believe this nonsense. It is one thing to fib politely in a customer presentation (where you are not exactly expected to speak the complete truth), and it is another thing entirely to build a business strategy on the same flimsy reasoning (to "inhale your own exhaust" as it is colorfully described). To our horror, in all too many cases, after mixing their marketing Kool-Aid they actually drink it.

In the last decade, this marketing fabrication process has spawned entire supporting industries in the form of testing programs that can give you quantified evaluations of your product designed so that again, you show up in the upper right-hand quadrant (or at least at the head of the class), regardless of how meaningless the necessary test metric used for comparison may be to actual customers. No one in business should be surprised by this. It is like an accountant asking you what you want the answer to be and then structuring the analysis so that is true. (We suspect that these service industry groups may have been hiring laid-off Enron or WorldCom accountants.) Of course, if you can buy the right answer, the same problems apply as before: the answer is not meaningful. We are not against marketers who spin stories to promote their new products. This is part of the game when dealing with creative and highly charged entrepreneurs. As insiders we enjoy seeing creativity at work. The "spun" truth is as OK as a polite lie, but can be deadly if you actually believe it.

In 1999 a group of bright engineers formed Abeona Networks, backed by $12 million of venture funding, and set out to build an exciting new product. Their initial look at the market suggested that the best use for their innovation was to accelerate transactions and save money on transaction processing systems. So they built that product, created marketing collateral showing how its transaction speed compared to the competition, even commissioned a testing lab that measured their performance and demonstrated their superiority. Despite the free advice that we gave them, they built their business on the assumption that their beliefs about what the market wanted were incontrovertibly true. Unfortunately, when show time came, customers did not buy the product, cash ran out, and Abeona was relegated to the Innovation Hall of Shame. As far as we could tell they never sought out experts who understood transaction systems, the business impact of slow transactions, and the common solutions for addressing these problems. Abeona presumed that if they built a better transaction gizmo (aka better mousetrap) the world would immediately reward them with orders. But that did not happen—the market reaction was unenthusiastic.

The moral is not that transaction speed is unimportant or that engineers cannot succeed by building smart widgets. But great engineering alone is not enough in today's business world, and failures all too often occur because the innovators did not adequately understand the customer's perspective and just how complicated the big picture is.

Engineers and software developers love to tackle difficult problems. Defining an intriguing problem creates a development challenge in and of itself. Once the technical team understood their development challenge, it was more fun to go out and tackle this tough problem than to understand the bigger picture of what customers wanted in terms of a solution viewed in the context of the rest of their systems. It would have cost less than $100,000 for Abeona to understand these issues early on. If they had done this work first, they would still have had $11,900,000 left to build a product that customers would buy.

THE GREAT ONE

Wayne Gretzky, "The Great One," was the Michael Jordan of hockey but he also revolutionized strategy, and what he accomplished carries a great lesson for today's business innovators. It all began when Gretzky's father told him the secret to success in hockey: "Don't skate to the puck; skate to where the puck is going!"

Skating to where the puck is *going* is a key strategy for business success in today's environment. You cannot just look at where your puck— market demand, money, whatever—is; you have to focus very intently on where it is going to be. "Skate to where the puck is going" is a simple, catchy, memorable phrase, but the devil, or God, is in the details. It is one thing to know you should be where the puck is going and another thing entirely to do it—otherwise Gretzky would not have towered above other hockey greats once his "secret" was leaked!

We can imagine a management consultant using this story as the key to his advice for a client, leading to head-slapping epiphany: "Of course! Where the puck is *going* to be! How could we have been so stupid?" The consultant then leaves, and as the euphoria dies down, the hapless client starts to wonder how he is going to know what the pucks in his business are and how to figure out where they are going.

In business, as in hockey, it is not what you know but what you do with your knowledge that counts. It is great to know you should go where the puck is going, but you have to first be clear about what the pucks are, and then learn how to predict their destinations. The three steps for doing this, the way you can implement our anticipation process, is the topic of this chapter.

In Step 1, you brainstorm the opportunities, listing all the possible alternatives, and then you discard the alternatives that have clear indicators of low value to narrow the options down to the ones worth focusing on.

In Step 2, you decide what is important to understand about each of these alternatives, determine the possible directions in which they may be heading, identify who the experts are that might be close enough to understanding the situation to increase your fact base, complete discussions with these experts to research each alternative to get the answers, and use that data to produce a preliminary ranking of the opportunities.

In Step 3, you explore what is involved in succeeding with each opportunity, deconstruct the alternative to reveal the actual customers that are key to its success, determine which plays are likely to score big, and then decide which of the alternatives present the best opportunities.

THE ANTICIPATION PROCESS

Step 1: Selecting the Alternatives

Extended group brainstorm. Use the people that care the most about your business to develop a master list of business alternatives that are available to you. We are assuming that the core group has thought through the alternatives that you can pursue more than anyone else, so this process represents the best possible starting point. Extend this brainstorming process to as many people as you can find who have relevant ideas and alternatives worth considering.

Eliminate the weakest ideas. Like any good brainstorming process, both good and bad ideas will result. In doing this work, you are always fighting for time, so the sooner that you eliminate the obviously bad ideas, the better. This is a good time to dump the dogs.

Determine the size of the remaining opportunities. Separate the remaining ideas into two or three piles. The most straightforward way to do this is to imagine if the alternative is wildly successful and then ask yourself how successful this idea can really become. Even if you just break the remaining opportunities into only two groups, one for the really big ideas and the other for the not as big ideas, at least you have developed some sort of priority.

Develop a knowledge base using electronic research. Spend a lot of time building a fact base through online searches so that you find out as much as you can about what is already known about the alternatives that you are researching. The more time you spend doing this, the more affective you will become later.

Create a database of experts. As you are building your fact base, begin creating a database of the individuals whose names come up as you are looking online. These names will form your initial expert database. You can expand on this database as you go along.

Step 2: Expert Interviews

Discussion guide. Before you begin your interviews, create a list of the topics and propose some of the questions that you might ask while you are having your expert discussions. You will not necessarily want to use every topic and every question with each person that you speak with, since the individuals that you will be speaking are probably going to have expertise in only part of the problem. But having a well-thought through set of topics should improve the quality of your interviews.

Alternative comparison matrix. As you go along, you will want to have some sort of scoring process that you can use to compare alternatives. In general, things like market opportunity size, ease of access, financial viability of the alterative, and competitive positioning are some of the factors that might help you identify strengths and weaknesses of the various alternatives.

Expert Interviews. This is the most fun and the most difficult part of the process. Starting with the names that you developed through electronic research, begin interviewing your experts. As you proceed, ask each expert for other names of people with whom you should speak.

Step 3: Ranking the Alternatives

Culling the best opportunities. As you get close to completing all of the interviews that you have planned, start ranking the alternatives using the framework of the comparison matrix developed earlier. How you end up forming the final ranking will be unique to the analysis that you are doing, but keep in mind, it helps if you simplify what you have found and develop visual aids to help transfer some of what you have learned through this process.

What's Worse than Not Knowing the Answer, Is Not Knowing the Question

A story is told about Peter Drucker, the legendary management consultant, by a happy client. He says that before an engagement with Drucker, they would send him lots of material about their business and problems. Then when Drucker showed up for the engagement, he would not give them any answers but rather would just ask them lots of questions. The day was spent with the clients answering the question (rather than being told the answers). The client found the process mysterious, having no doubt that the experience was highly valuable, but finding it surprising that they had all the answers. The issue was asking the right questions.

We have found this to be true in our own consulting business. We begin every assignment with a preliminary phase during which we ask our client's management team lots and lots of questions to understand their perceptions and interpretation of the business. We have found that they have most of the critical data already; we can help by focusing on the right questions and then expanding their fact base by talking with people outside their companies.

Here is one of our favorite examples about the importance of the question. The company: United Airlines. As the era of the Internet blossomed, United finally got a rude awakening concerning how it was about to impact their business. Travel sites on the Web made it really easy to shop for flights (much easier than it had ever been before, especially given that travel agents were not really the impartial advocates for the customer—they got a part of the airfare as compensation). If United did nothing, they could see that they were going to end up being really marginalized with a nasty impact on profits, so they aggressively moved to develop their frequent flyer Web site with the intention of leveraging their Mileage Plus brand and customer loyalty into participation on a travel portal site.

United spent a lot of time trying to understand wireless access to the Internet from a personal digital assistant (PDA) or an Internet mobile phone. They knew that their highest value business customers were also early adopters and users of this kind of advanced communication technology. What could be done to make the Internet phone or PDA into a valuable part of the travel portal? We have all had images of a stressed out traveler finding out his flight is delayed and using his PDA to find a new flight, and then rushing off to the gate to make a connection without a minute to spare. But as reasonable as this sounds, it is not actually what most people really wanted or needed. United made a huge effort and made much progress technically, but had very limited success in gaining users. While the idea of a stressed out executive making a connection by seconds produces a great mental image, United eventually found out that they were better off trying to serve the mainstream user. Finally they had the critical epiphany; they started to understand what the right question was. They realized simply that the customer—the business traveler—had little interest in using technology just for technology's sake. The need was to do travel planning as simply and as fast as possible. The cell phone was clearly a wonderful device; if your travel plans changed you could pick up your cell phone, immediately call the United travel agent, and rebook your flights. In fact, many of today's PDAs have phones built into them, so if United only sent you an alert via e-mail, all you would have to do is to push a button on your PDA to dial United's reservation agents. Sweet. United perceived great value if that transaction could be moved to the PDA (agent calls are expensive), but finally understood that given the limited displays and marginal data bandwidth that was typical, they were a long way from being able to make the wireless transaction faster than the agent transaction, and until that happened it was completely unrealistic to expect anyone to use it. All the user cared about was speed and simplicity. Whether or not such wireless transactions can ever be fast enough is still an open question, so United has focused its wireless efforts on areas like using e-mail to send flight change information to customers automatically, something that does work well, while leaving the more complex transactions to phone agents. Understanding this was a matter of finding the right question to ask.

It is our belief that had United asked the right questions to the right experts early on, they would have figured out what they needed to do. They would have saved a few years of struggling down the wrong path and might have used the several millions of dollars they spent much more productively. All of their research and development did not lead them to the right answer. Discovering that wireless PDAs were good for sending alerts but not good for doing complex reservations is not rocket science. This sort of knowledge comes from knowing what and whom to ask.

DEMAND ANTICIPATION

Knowing where and how to move starts with identifying the alternatives that appear to hold the most promise. The goal of business is usually to sell a product or service, so we will start by looking at alternatives in terms of business opportunities. Each alternative is an opportunity that eventually will have an outcome, a strategic initiative that you can take, along with a clear understanding of its possible results. The alternatives are the choices that you are making—markets, products, channel, campaigns, partners, acquisitions, and other decisions that you are considering as part of your business plan.

At the outset, when you are building your business plan, you are faced with these key questions:

- Which alternatives (opportunities) should you spend time examining, with whom and why?
- Where are these alternatives heading?
- How will demand materialize along the way?
- Why do customers care, and what do they value?
- What is the demand-side view of the opportunity?
- What is the time frame?

It is at this point that you wish you knew more about what was going to happen in the future because, if you were able to look ahead, you would end up creating a better business strategy.

Understanding future demand is so valuable you might well think everyone already does it, but it is done remarkably infrequently. To a surprising degree, companies explore demand empirically. They pick some target markets, expend considerable marketing and sales effort to go after them, see what works, and then act, without first trying to answer some basic questions. This costs a huge amount of money, and, worse yet, it takes a lot of time—and time is something that innovative companies do not have enough of. When we ask the principals in those companies why they do it that way, they look bewildered and say, "Isn't that what marketing and sales people do? Isn't that how they work?" Maybe it is what they do, but that does not make it right. There is a strong belief—a very damaging one in our opinion—that, since the stuff they are working on is so new, trial and error is the best way of proceeding because no one really knows what is going to happen anyway.

We start with the belief that, in fact, there are people out there who understand the situations you are about to face. We think that the problem is a different one than you might think. The problem is not that there are no people to talk to; it is just that they are hard to find. The difficulty with trying to anticipate where demand is headed comes from the fact that innovation trends often are "under the radar" of most observers. Things that have the potential to significantly influence the future are often unnoticed as they are incubating, and the people that know the most about the future are, likewise, under the radar and hard to identify. It is not that these people do not exist, it is just that the general consensus is not yet aware of the innovation or its potential impact. With any important innovation, it takes time before the general public becomes aware of it. During its incubation period, there are people with an understanding of an innovation's potential. However, there might not be many of these people, and it is likely that they may not have a broad understanding of the impact of the innovation. A key element of our anticipation process is to seek out these people (we are calling them experts) and understand their perspective on the innovation and its potential. The Internet is a good example of this phenomenon.

Waiting until an innovation surfaces and the general consensus catches up with it before you move is always better than not watching and not changing, but it is a very inefficient and expensive way to discover demand. It takes lots of time and money, and when you finally get an idea after all the trial and error, you have lost time-to-market and momentum. And when you use trial and error, by the time you get the right answer it is often too late.

Suppose you could improve your chances of business success by focusing on the opportunities with the greatest potential. Your future vision does not have to be perfect for there to be high value in this approach. You do not have to decide what the absolute best opportunity is, you just have to decide which ones not to waste time on, a much easier decision. Imagine that you are able to identify the majority of the top opportunities and best customers for your innovative new product well before it is ready to be released to the market. This limited focus improves your chances of succeeding by a huge amount. Besides, the earlier you can anticipate the right answer, the greater the ability you have to test that decision every day with the people you meet and the questions you ask.

When you are an industry analyst, you see lots of business plans and watch many teams go through the process of bringing innovative new products and services into the market. A common thread across many of these situations is that many teams are content to postpone their understanding of which markets will be the most receptive to their innovations and why. Time and time again, executive teams wait until their products are market ready before they begin engaging customers. We think that market segments, killer applications, value propositions, key customers, and leading users should be known at the outset, concurrent with the design of their innovation. We are amazed when companies do not do even the most simplistic forms of market sizing in the early days of working on their innovation. We wonder how it is possible to spend millions on the development of a new product without simultaneously understanding the size of the market opportunity.

Think about the process of getting a reference account for a new product. Without reference users, innovative new products could never get to market. So you know that you are going to need a reference customer before you even begin working on your product. Furthermore, if you have a "really big" idea, the "next new thing," then the customer base you will be building will be vast, so it is only natural that you will need to produce some reference accounts that substantiate this idea. In other words, before you set out to build your new product, you should already have a really good idea of who the first users of the product will have to be. Then why, we ask, do innovation teams so often fail to recruit big name reference users at the earliest possible stage of their design and development? Finding and then pitching the right person at a big potential reference account is the thing to do—and it should be done as early in the process as possible. Tell him that you think his company will find great value in your new product and you will offer incentives that add value—implementation support, onsite back-up, whatever it takes—to get them to be beta testers or early adopters. And if you cannot get top tier reference accounts, maybe there is something wrong with your strategy.

It never ceases to amaze us how many times companies showing us their newest technologies have some incredibly lame reference accounts. Here they are, telling us about the greatest inventions ever to hit the planet, and when we ask them who their first customers are they tell us about a Romanian welfare agency or car dealership in Podunk, Arkansas. Once someone told us that the United Nations was their big reference account. Now that might sound great, but the big problem with having the United Nations as a reference account is that it is sort of a "one of a kind" type of institution. There is not another enterprise like it. It is hard to figure out how you can make a living off a market of one. The reason we have so much trouble believing companies with weak reference accounts is that the lack of good references commensurate with the type of market a company is trying to build shows us that the company probably never even tried to develop strong first users early on in the development cycle. And if they have not done that, then there is likely to be a bunch of other things wrong with what they are telling us. Or, to put it in simpler terms, "I smell a rat." Getting reference accounts early that substantiates the business plan seems to us to be a perfectly natural thing to do. Just like you would not design a new computer without a power supply, you should not build something unless you have a pretty good idea who the first users are going to be. You do not have to have all the answers. But you should have thought this thing through to the point where, early on, you have gone to a few of the perfect first users that you want and have recruited them to become part of the process.

In the same way that you address the issues of identifying and recruiting the right reference accounts early on, you can use the same logic to sort through other issues like your route to market. (If your innovation is really top notch, then your sales channel should reflect that, should it not? Asking top-level people in the sales channel about what they consider to be the most important issues surrounding your innovation may save you months of gathering the same information empirically.) And you can do the same for other targets of your strategic plan—business partnerships, investors, advisors.

The ability to sort out the future and focus on the best opportunities—where the puck is going—is what differentiated Gretzky from less talented hockey players. Gretzky knew that he had to find a better way to position himself to set up a scoring opportunity because there were not many in a typical hockey game. He had to make the most of the opportunities that did occur. Similarly, there are not many opportunities to score big victories with new products, so we knew there had to be a better way to position corporations to foresee the future. We call our process simple Demand Anticipation. There are four basic concepts:

1. Be clear about precisely what you are trying to understand (the alternatives that you care most about and the questions that you want to answer).
2. Pick the people (the experts) who can help you the most answering those questions.
3. Talk to as many of those experts as possible.
4. Synthesize the answers you get to create a forecast (or prediction) of what will happen.

Anticipating the future—seeing where your alternatives will lead—is not as difficult or mysterious as you might think. In fact, after you use the Demand Anticipation process just a few times, you will be able to do this kind of forward-looking investigation like a pro. It puts you in the middle of the decision-making process where the game is decided and forces you to understand and integrate all the key actions, including your customer's perspective and taking measure of the competition. When you are done, you will have a clear, comprehensive view of the future and discover it is not so hard to see where the alternatives are leading. It is like the moment in an airplane when all of a sudden what you see puts everything into perspective—you see where your home is as you fly over it. This anticipation process combines three disciplines—market research, forecasting, and strategic planning—and has three steps:

1. brainstorming the set of possible market opportunities, discarding the weakest opportunities and developing a preliminary sizing of the remaining opportunities;

2. identifying and interviewing experts who are directly involved with the applications that form the foundation for each of the opportunities being considered and, using our six criteria (strength of need, value proposition, potential volume, completeness of product offering, sales channel, positioning), to rank the comparative strengths of these opportunities; and

3. for the highest-ranking opportunities, develop the dream team of customers, business partners, and channel partners that are essential for the ultimate winner in the market to attract and elicit all of the information you can from them.

There are four elements of our anticipation process: (a) you probably already know 80% of the answer right now without studying it, you just need to reveal it in a simpler form, (b) much of the information that you need is with the *first buyers, first sellers, first integrators (consultants, experts . . .) and first distributors* in the industry, go talk to them and find out what they're doing to solve the problems you're looking at. Throw away any advice you have gathered from people who are not really involved with your subject matter; they do not know. Also do not water down your fact base by adding information from nonbuyers and nonusers to the mix; there is little important information there, (c) find out who has the potential to buy your product in the future—especially who will spend the majority of the money on it, and (d) find the killer app—the function that customers most value—and then either deliver that killer app or butt up against it so closely that you get sucked in as part of the process of acquiring that application. The anticipation process helps you to focus on these four elements and incorporates research type practices into the strategic planning process.

FIVE QUESTIONS

A key part of anticipating the future is to formulate the right questions. While each situation dictates a unique set of questions, there are five that we use as starting points:

1. Over the past five years, which businesses had successes that most closely compare to the success that you are expecting?

2. Imagine that your new product is a big success, who is your best customer and what would he tell an associate about the single most important reason you brought value to them?

3. What is the single most important question that you need to answer right now to improve your chances for success?

4. If you had a magic wand, what factors would you change about your company or product?

5. What word or phrase do you want to "own" in the minds of your customers because it best embodies the potential value that you hold?

We have found these questions useful as discussion starters. We find it important to get managers to paint their vision of the future for us. Since what they are doing is important, we want to hear about the impact that it will have. Getting a team to share this with us generates all sorts of ideas for where we need to look for more information. Each future scenario forms a hypothesis. In turn, this allows us to consider ways to get more evidence to either prove or disprove each hypothesis. This is our way to figure out how to get more facts that can help us (and them) anticipate the future. The teams with the largest fact bases are the ones that are in the best position to anticipate the future.

THE DO-IT-YOURSELF FORECAST

A hockey game generates a lot of effort and action but only twenty to thirty shots on goal per game with about 10 percent of those shots scoring. In business, the scoring opportunities are also limited and just as risky, because if you do not score, sooner or later you run out of time, money, and resources. Hockey fans recognize the importance of each shot in a game. Goals in business are just as important but the fact is, as in hockey, shots are often missed. All too often, we do not give all of our scoring opportunities the same importance, but we should. Picking your shots and then making each one as effective as possible are crucial to the outcome. And if you are going to pick your shots, you have to have some idea about what is about to happen. Business people have a word for doing just that—forecasting.

An important part of our anticipation process is to develop a forecast of business potential. In its simplest form, a forecast is a visual representation of a collection of facts that you have regarding a business opportunity. When you have few facts, it will be a crude representation. As you learn more about these opportunities, your forecast improves.

There are many variables to sort out in producing an initial forecast, but the most important single factor is the strength of customer demand. Technology, competition, regulation, and economics all play a role, but customer demand ultimately decides your fate, and customer buying events (dollars spent, units purchased, and so on) should be the vertical axis in your forecast.

For the timescale of your forecast, the horizontal axis, you need to anticipate what customers will be doing over the short term—eighteen to thirty-six months (not the next five to ten years). If you think that it takes about eighteen months to develop and bring a new product in your category to market, then you should try to forecast the market for a period of about thirty-six months. Any longer than that takes you into a period of time that is more than two development cycles away, too far out to care about. It is extremely valuable to anticipate what will happen in the next eighteen to thirty-six months when you will measure the results of the decisions you make and the actions you take now.

For the opportunities that interest innovators the most, the forecast that you need will not be in the *Wall Street Journal* or *Business Week*. By the time the general awareness of these markets has grown enough to interest the readership of the business media, the real innovations have already begun to take hold. It is a given that at the outset you will not have much data with which to work. The first time through the process of forecasting the business opportunity you will have to make some assumptions and maybe do a little guessing. That is why we call it the "do it yourself" forecast. We think that the first step is to answer these questions:

1. Will there be more, fewer, or the same number of products like this bought in the next twelve months when compared to the past twelve? What about for the next twenty-four months?

2. If the answer is "more," about how much more—five times, ten times, fifty times?

3. What are the reasons why demand goes up? Are there any barriers or obstacles that must be surmounted before demand increases?

4. What other events have to happen before demand goes up? How long will it take before these occur?

5. And if the market is not going to grow rapidly in the near term, when will there be a significant increase, and what will cause that growth spurt to happen?

In other words, where is the knee in the curve? At a very high level, how does demand increase over the foreseeable future, when does it start to spike upward, and about how high will it reach if everything goes perfectly well?

Understand the answers to these questions and you will understand a lot. You can make some broad assumptions initially, but as you do you will start to discover some things you would like to know more about. To get these answers, you need more input. It is not a question of locking yourself up in a room and making up an answer. Initially you can do some electronic research and other secondary research to learn a bit more. After that, you need to talk to experts—people who are totally immersed in the problems that you are planning to solve.

The people you need to talk to are not average customers or the man on the street. To learn the secrets of baseball, you would talk first to the great players, not the hopefuls in the minor leagues. The premise is the same in business. We often say that to find the experts that you are looking for you have got to go to the "scene of the crime" of an application. Just as a police detective always goes to the crime scene to develop a perspective of the crime he is trying to solve, so you have got to find experts who are at the "scene of the application"—the ones who are fully immersed in trying to apply innovative solutions to specific applications of interest. The key sources of insight are the leading-edge customers—the people who have been trying to solve the problem you are working on using whatever techniques they can. If you can talk to twenty-five of the most advanced users, people who are trying to gain an unfair business advantage in the area, you will learn a great deal.

The idea is simple—the execution is more challenging:

- It helps to have lots of contacts, networks you can leverage directly and indirectly.
- It helps to know how the important market segments are structured.
- It helps to mine the Web for the people you need.
- It helps to search out conferences and other venues where experts might come together.

We will give you ways of finding those individuals later. You will have to find and talk with them, which may sound like another impossible task, but it is not.

The target experts are busy people who use their time wisely. Why should they talk to you or anyone else for that matter? Often they end up talking to you simply because you share a passion with them, a very important bond. They are interested in the same field—as a customer rather than as a supplier—and are eager to discuss it with someone else who is knowledgeable and can help them understand it better. Identifying and getting through to these individuals requires some craft and patience, but it is more than possible and provides an invaluable source of critical information and perspective.

We find that human nature acts in our favor when we ask someone to share his or her opinions with us. We live in an increasingly stressful world. Everyone is so busy getting his or her work done that having someone actually ask you for your opinion about an interesting subject is refreshing. You know how it is—you go to work and your co-workers are all running around, your managers are all stressed out and too busy to listen, you go home and your family is too busy to ask you for anything other than your car keys and some money for gas. So when someone actually starts a sentence with "I'd like to understand your opinion about" you go—wow, that is really cool, someone actually wants to know what I think!

Yes, it is hard work to complete the expert discussions that you will need. No doubt about it. But once you start doing it you will be glad you did. You will end up expanding your fact base enormously, and that, itself, will become a competitive advantage. In the final phase you will synthesize this information, and you will have the answers you need. You will know which ideas are important, start moving to act on them, and get ready to take advantage of the opportunities you have identified.

VOODOO MARKET RESEARCH?

At this point, market researchers—the people whose minions call you at home at dinnertime—get nervous and starting asking questions:

- Is not the process we just described exactly the kind of bad thinking we got warned about in Stat 101 in college (making inferences from too little data)?
- Is it not sheer madness or "voodoo market research" to think that you can determine important and unknown market trends with just a handful of discussions?

- What about giant surveys and statistically significant percentages, or at least focus groups?

Expensive, comprehensive, statistically precise market research studies are fine for refining marketing strategies for cigarettes or predicting the outcome of an election. But they do not play an important role in the *anticipation* process for a simple reason: If you want to learn about something important by talking to people, you have to talk to people about something that they know. For the kind of disruptive innovation brought about by interesting new products, only a few people may have an informed opinion.

Average consumers can help you understand the simple things about a market: how many people buy things like that, what the average selling price is, what segments buy the most and why. That is the kind of information you generally do not have to get yourself because it is part of conventional wisdom. Usually, sources like the *Wall Street Journal* or trade publications have what you will need to understand these aspects. But only experts involved in the area that you are working on can help you understand the future. Adding more samples to the database does not help if the additional people do not know enough about the problem. To summarize, deciding what to do based on twenty-five discussions is either idiocy (not enough data points) or brilliant, if these twenty-five happen to be a third of all the experts around.

Stent Wars

Anticipation is a big factor in the healthcare industry since new drugs and procedures must go through a lengthy Food and Drug Administration (FDA) approval cycle under the watchful eyes of both competitors and investors. It is not unusual for the first product winning approval to ultimately use its lead to capture the largest market share. In 2003, a big battle was waging between Johnson & Johnson and Boston Scientific in the multibillion dollar drug-coated stent market (drug-coated stents keep coronary arteries open more successfully and much longer than plain metal devices, reducing the need for repeated angioplasties and for heart bypass surgery). Boston Scientific knew that its approval would lag Johnson & Johnson's by at least six months, but correctly anticipated market conditions that could present enough of an opportunity to quickly turn demand in its favor. Johnson & Johnson left several openings by antagonizing doctors with inconsistent inventory practices, predatory pricing, failure to provide a variety of sizes, and having an inferior delivery system (to insert the stent during the medical procedure). Meanwhile, while Boston Scientific was completing its FDA approval cycle, it anticipated the opportunity created by its competitor's shortsightedness and designed a comprehensive launch by combining its stent's higher efficacy results, reasonable pricing model, advanced delivery system, and availability in several sizes, backed by sufficient inventory to propel it into a market leadership position.

Coffee Break?

It is pretty common that, as part of the work we do, we have to forecast the future. We've made a number of "right on" calls about how technology markets would evolve and lots of people wonder whether we're really good or just really lucky. (We've also made some pretty bad calls, which thanks to our aging memories, we can't seem to remember.) Well, we're going to share our "secret sauce" with you. The truth is that we owe a lot to the fortuitous circumstances of our office location. We're located in the tony town of Los Altos tucked in besides Palo Alto and Mountain View. Our office is right across the street from that famous Los Altos Silicon Valley hobnobbing landmark—Peet's Coffee Shop. And of course you know that Peet's strong caffeine brew is preferred above Starbucks by Silicon Valley's elite and their spouses. Now after watching the scene at Peet's for all these years we came up with an amazing cross correlation between the traffic at Peet's and the economy of the valley. There are three indicators that we've developed: How long is the "on the way to work" line before 8 AM? What type of cars do the spouses drive when they get their lattes during the 10AM to 12PM shift after dropping the kiddies at school? And how many bicyclists appear in their colorful spandex in the 2PM to 4PM slot? Our big breakthrough in this research was when we discovered that the biker index was really made up of job searchers taking their afternoon breaks. So when the lines are long in the early morning, the Boxters are parked in front in the late morning and there are few bikers at the end of the day, the valley economy is roaring. Short lines, too many dinged vans and packs of bikers, we've got a recession. That's our secret. All the rest of the research we do is just icing on the coffee cake. The only hard part of this is all the caffeine we consume to keep this index fresh!

As we've mentioned, we find that a process of first describing and then interpreting future success reveals a lot:

What is the need? Why will customers care? Probably one of the most important things to do is to refine your understanding of buying motivations. What need must you fill? Why will customers care? Looking at it through this process gives you the ability to focus on what the most important customers are trying to accomplish.

What is the value? You will be doing more than filling a need. Most likely, customers will derive value in several ways. What are the buying motivations that will drive customers to want what you are doing? How much will they pay for it?

How large is the potential market and which market segments are most important? If your idea meets with widespread acceptance, how big is the market potential? Which markets will get interested soonest and why?

What are the complete customer requirements? What else, in addition to what you do, will customers need to get the full satisfaction from what you do?

Which business partners are important? Which business partners are needed to make this success scenario come about? How critical are these partners to the eventual success of this alternative?

What are the sales channels? How do customers get informed? How does this success scenario will be play out on the sales side? How do customers learn about new products? How long is the sales cycle? How long will it take for the best customers to get on board with your product, and what is the best way of approaching them?

How formidable is the competition? Which competitors will be the biggest threats and what are the competitive barriers to entry? As part of the brainstorming you should go through a process of determining which competitors you were selling against and, looking at this from the customer's perspective, why you won the business.

Remember, we are asking you to look at the future eighteen to twenty-four months from now, not five years away. This is an important point, because it is much easier to predict what will be going on in your industry in the shorter term than in the longer term. Also, there are many resources available to support you in this process since most industry analysis is done on an eighteen- to twenty-four-month horizon. Going much further out in time complicates this sort of forecasting analysis in three major respects. First, in today's markets there is too much volatility to anticipate out sixty months; second, the planning horizon for most companies closely matches their development cycles, which generally are less than twenty-four months, and finally the market conditions that you are most able to influence are within the next twenty-four months (influencing market conditions further out usually means you have to first successfully establish a base).

After you have completed this brainstorming process for the first alternative in your table, it is time to move on to the rest of the alternatives, repeating the process for each. The goal of this process is to understand the potential of each of the alternatives that you are considering and to get an idea of the degree of difficulty you may encounter on the way to achieving success.

When you brainstorm about the future of an alternative and develop its "best case scenario," there are a lot of significant clues that come up as you play out the story. These are clues in that they tell you some of the obstacles that you will have to hurdle to achieve the success you are looking for. One of the most difficult things to figure out is an understanding of the customer's perspective on the complete set of elements needed to get the value you are talking about—not just the things that you do but everything else standing between your customer and the total value the alternative will bring to him or her. Too often companies see the world from their own perspective and think that customers have nothing better to do than to complete what they do not do. Just like an auto engine is not any good without the car body and a lot more, more than likely what you do will need a set of complementary products and services in order for your customers to benefit. Playing out these scenarios will help give you an idea of how your customers can benefit the most, what else they have got to do to achieve this, and how long it might take them to figure all of this out.

This sort of forecasting is not something that is just done by innovative companies looking to understand where their world is headed. It is pretty common for football coaches to go through a similar process before a big game. Teams hire scouts to go to their competitors' games to report back on their strengths and weaknesses. They will also subscribe to independent scouting services, they will read sports analysts, and they will even listen to fan input in order to get an idea of what they are coming up against. In practice sessions before big games they might deploy one of their squads in the attack formation that their competitors favor, just to give their players a look at what they will be facing. This type of anticipation is pretty common in sports. The process that we are describing transfers these concepts to businesses.

Unfavorable or Unexpected Market Conditions?

Even though they received $38 million from leading technology venture investors, Wincom Systems could not get enough customers to buy their expensive, high-speed switching server to create a viable business. The product was costly to engineer because of the custom silicon parts they had designed for it. When Wincom shut their doors and returned what cash they had left to investors, it was blamed on "market conditions."

That is an interesting spin: If you build a product for which there is no market, is that a market condition problem? The Irridium satellite phone failed because their target user, global business travelers, did not want a phone that could not be used inside a building or in a car. Is that a market condition problem or a dumb product? When we visited Wincom—more than a year before they eventually shut down and in plenty of time to make important course corrections—it was very clear to us that the market conditions were unfavorable. How could we know so much? Was this just a lucky voodoo marketing goat-entrails reading? We had an unfair advantage. We have been covering these markets longer than anyone else—we are constantly talking to customers, service providers, channel members, and vendors. We do not claim to know how to do all the dirty little engineering that is needed to make this sort of stuff work, we do know about what customers buy and why—them pesky market conditions.

Did they listen to us when we gave them free advice about what they needed to do to capture the market? Not one word! They could not move us out the door fast enough. Like many other companies building exotic engineering solutions that failed to win customer acceptance, Wincom blamed it on the market.

To a remarkable degree, the high-tech industry blames the whole post–dot-com recession on market conditions. Times were certainly tough (especially compared to the preceding insanity when it did not take much to fund a wacko company or sell crackpot products). But, we cannot help but recall Charles Kettering's famous 1930s recession quote from a keynote address to a group of business innovators, "I believe business will come back when we get some products that people want to buy." Kettering, the inventor of the electric car-starter, founder of Delco, and head of GM's research labs to 1947, after he sold Delco to United Motors which GM acquired in 1918, was one of the leading technologists in the early half of the twentieth century. As Kettering aptly pointed out, the best way out of a recession is to make products that people want to buy.

In the same speech, Kettering also said, "Research is simply to find out what you are going to do when you can't keep on doing what you are doing now." A lot of companies have a challenge like the one Wincom faced. The world of technology is still rapidly changing—products that made perfect sense twenty-four months ago may have little relevance today. As Wincom proved, rather painfully, you cannot keep doing what you are doing just because a bunch of engineers want to solve a difficult problem.

Chapter 5

Big Plays

You need chaos in your soul to give birth to a dancing star.
—Friedrich Nietzsche

Dancing with Elephants

When he took the helm at IBM, Lou Gerstner made a big play. He decided to defy expectations by refusing to break up the giant corporation into dozens of baby IBMs, each of which would serve a different market. Breaking the company up was a decision that had seemed all but made. IBM's board had made it clear that this was the direction they endorsed. Gerstner, however, foresaw that customers would need comprehensive integration skills to deliver new technology to their clients—technology that would improve their businesses and allow them the flexibility demanded by a rapidly changing marketplace. This was a direction that his competitors—and many at his own company—did not see. By anticipating where the market was heading, Gerstner transformed the very future of his company. A true visionary, he saw that only IBM was in a position to focus a vast array of systems, technologies, and services on the really big problems facing businesses of all sizes. He saw what the aggregation of these technologies under a single brand would mean. His decision was based on the seeing just far enough ahead to determine that this was the single biggest sustainable difference that IBM had to offer. He led IBM by anticipating that the market would need a provider capable of managing complex technology integration.

Stuck Share

In the innovation business, we often fail to see that we are in a situation where market share is stuck for factors that may be beyond our control and that what is needed is to quickly adopt strategies to compensate. Sometime in the 1970s the big oil companies marketing gasoline to consumers came up with an important strategic realization: It was really difficult to shift market share. A movement of even a single percentage point was a big event. Making that happen was expensive and would probably cost more to achieve than the profits from that shift would bring. The reasons for this are pretty simple—gas stations have a fixed location and the typical consumer driving patterns in most communities were established by the local highway systems. Brand advertising was important, but all of the major oil companies had achieved a sort of parity with their brand recognition and positioning. An oil company's cost structure was pretty much set by a combination of the price of oil and the processing and delivery network needed to bring their products to the local market. Gasoline marketing differed from other consumer marketing in one fundamental way: There were enormous barriers to shifting market share. It was not like the Coke versus Pepsi battles, where consumers could easily switch products. The result was that oil companies that wanted to grow their retail businesses had to resort to "big plays": (1) buying or selling hundreds of gas stations in order to reallocate retail operations to get more efficiencies—in other words, dump stations in markets where you had a weak infrastructure and buy stations in markets where you had some sort of economic advantage, and (2) sell more than just gas to increase revenues—move into the convenience store and fast food businesses. Today, big storage companies like EMC are facing similar market conditions. It is difficult to shift market share because it is difficult and expensive for customers to change storage platforms.

WRAPPER

An essential part of succeeding in the market with most innovative new products and services is something we are calling the big play. The big play can be the vehicle that makes the innovation have real impact. It is the springboard for pushing your idea to a higher operating level. Or the big play can be the "wrapper" that is needed to attract sufficient interest and financing to move the innovation from the drawing boards into customers' hands. By their nature, innovations cause change. Change causes disruptions. And potential disruptions create market conditions that are ripe for big plays. Our definition of a big play is that combination of product innovation, business model, financing, route to market, and complete product offering that maximizes investment return over a relatively short time.

A truly "big" play changes the rules of the game. This is what the oil companies found necessary to do when they were in their "stuck share" phase. In Hollywood, a new big play that may now be taking shape is the idea of selling shares in individual movie projects. If successful, it will challenge—and eventually change—all of the rules of the film industry game. No one has ever done it before, and therefore the idea generates a buzz that allows it to leap barriers more cautious business will try to erect.

We use the word "wrapper" to describe an affect that a big play can have on a business opportunity. It is a good term for trying to convey that innovators often get an opportunity to redefine the business landscape in ways that suit them. Henry Ford's vision of a car for every family is a good example of how the "bigness" of his idea was a wrapper that propelled a whole chain of events from assembly-line manufacturing and a nationwide dealership network to the financing plan for constructing the factories.

We are often confronted with situations where a start-up team has been beaten to a pulp by a board of directors hell-bent on trying to turn a profit that, in turn, forces them to make short-term decisions that are not in their own best interest. These are situations where the team has lost site of their big play and have instead become the managers of a small business. The right thing for many of these companies to do is to push against the desire for short-term profitability and instead get back in touch with the big idea that brought them to where they were in the first place. Investment in innovation is not an activity designed to create a bunch of marginally profitable small businesses. It is a different game, a game where big plays can result in big returns.

The big play is particularly difficult to discuss because there is no really simple way to describe it. You know it when you see it. Catalysts speed up chemical reactions. In a parallel manner, a big play can act as an accelerator for bringing an innovation to reality. Yet no one has devised a test to determine the "bigness" of an idea. And different situations may warrant different approaches. There is only so much that we can describe in a general way. We cannot tell you here how to create the big play that your particular business needs. That is something you will have to figure out on your own. But we can motivate you to spend time thinking about potential big plays for your business, to develop the concept of the big play, and to begin executing it. Even if we cannot describe the big plays that you will need for your specific business, we do know what the elements are. Big plays combine the ingredients of product, distribution, business partnerships, and financing into a stew that lets an innovator quickly gain market share and leverage in a given business sector.

Poster Boy Marketing

Inktomi was the brainchild of a UC Berkeley computer science professor and his star student whose research work focused on "clustering"—how you could aggregate large numbers of computers to work on a common task, something that has been done recently with amazingly good results in astronomy. They saw the opportunity, but they also knew cool—their name was cool, their logo was cool, and their technology exotic—and therefore very cool. But their basic product focus, caching, was completely obscure. To create attention for their company, Inktomi orchestrated such an effective public relations campaign that the fact that almost no one understood what their products was for did not matter. In spring 1998, in rapid-fire sequence, Inktomi announced Sun Microsystems as a major partner/investor, the availability of their product, its poster boy first customer (AOL!), and that they were going to be taken public almost immediately by one of Wall Street's most prestigious firms. Within a few days, the company had gone from being an obscure tech company with an unpronounceable and unspellable name to the "I think I need to know about these guys" category. After all, if AOL and big Wall Street firms were interested, it must to be important. A little theater brought a huge return— Hollywood would have been proud!

TURNING RED LIGHTS TO GREEN

When you leave your house in the morning to commute to work, you are probably going to encounter some traffic lights along the way. Some are green, others are red. While the red lights may delay you a bit, you would not think of going back home just because you hit a red light. Red lights are just one of the temporary obstacles that you encounter in the normal course of your commute. They are something that you just put up with on a daily basis. But what if you could do something that would turn these red lights to green so that when you left in the morning you would be guaranteed in advance that you would have a smooth commute? Who would not want that?

Well, that is the role of the "big play." It is your way of easing the path of your innovation so that, as it progresses along the normal route, opportunities unfold in front of you that simplify everything you do. A big play establishes the big picture of what your innovation is able to accomplish. It explains why the time and money invested will yield not just an important new product but a whole new way of satisfying a really important need.

INVESTORS EXPECT A LOT

You do not have to go far to look for examples of how the system is supporting the concept of big plays. It happens in venture investing all the time. The whole concept of a round of venture funding is tied to the fact that investors who put money in a company expect that the valuation of the company will rise significantly over the short life of the investment. In other words, investors putting $10 million into a start-up whose overall valuation is $25 million expect that in a short time—perhaps eighteen to twenty-four months—the start-up will succeed in increasing its valuation to $100 million. So investors expect the start-up to pull off some sort of small miracle by increasing its valuation four times in a very short period. But that is the way the game is played. This significant change in valuation provides a clear way to judge the potential success of a strategic plan. Are the strategies being considered capable of producing such a large increase in valuation over a short period?

This is also why we spend so much time whining about companies that are content just to make a profit. Over the years we have seen many venture-backed companies come around and proudly tell us that they are on the verge of being profitable. Too often, these companies have thrown away any chances of major success they have had by sacrificing investment in their future for the short-term balancing of their financial statements. Sure, they may appear to be on the verge of being profitable, but they may have decimated their engineering and development teams to do it. They have essentially lost their inspiration and their ability to pull off that big play.

It is amazing to us how many times this happens. A company comes in showing off their latest widget. They tell us that they have their new product coming into the market, and they have signed up five customers for it although they are not allowed to tell us the names of any of these customers. They expect to be profitable in "just a few months." To save time, we have a sign on our conference room wall that runs through the pitch for them, all they have got to do is fill in the blanks: "We raised _____ million dollars a year ago, developed this _____ new product, hired some sales people a few months ago and we've got really good customers _____ and _____, although you may not have heard of any of them, you can trust us that they're really important customers who just love using our product and we expect to be profitable in _____ months." What they generally do not like to tell us is that they had to lower their prices significantly to get these first users, and, by the way, there are only a handful of engineers left at the company because now they are putting their energies into marketing and selling. And they are upset when we do not jump out of our chairs and do back flips when they give us their big spiel. Bringing a new product into the market is not the goal in and of itself. As we have been saying, in today's markets, having a product is just the starting point; everyone who wants to seems to be able to get the money it takes to do basic product development. We are looking for the *bigness* of the idea, the one idea that will change an entire way of doing business.

A big idea has a lot going for it; the product is just the beginning. Big ideas come with all the trimmings—big customers (really big customers), big market opportunities, top-tier investors, well-thought-through channel plans, first-class engineering teams, imaginative business models, and for start-ups, a well-understood set of exit options—the works.

You can look to Hollywood for examples of where the concept of the big play has almost become institutionalized. It is only natural for studio executives looking at a new script to focus on the potential return they will get for an investment in the project. Today, the fates of most movies are determined by their opening weekend box-office tallies: How many screens does the movie open on and how many tickets are sold? That, in turn, drives the questions:

1. What is going to pull (or push) moviegoers to the opening weekend—star appeal, plot, special effects, and so on? (This is Hollywood's version of differentiation and positioning—show us how you are different and who is going to care about it.)

2. What is the audience demographic for the single largest component of moviegoers (teenage boys, twenty somethings, and so on)? (If what you are doing is unique, who is going to buy what you are making and why?);

3. What will the trailer look like? (How do you expect to market and sell your product in a way that takes advantage of your differentiation?)

Just as studios evaluate the potential of a new movie by considering its bigness factors, you can evaluate the potential for your own innovation by looking at your bigness factors in advance and doing what you can to build on them.

1. How big is the market and how fast is it changing?

2. How are you different and how can you sustain your differentiation?

3. How does your business model let you take advantage of the market?

We once ran into a movie executive who worked in international film distribution. Every year he had to select the twenty-five independent films that his company would market in foreign countries. He told us that the secret to his success was never to watch the films. Instead, he would pour through the marketing material created to market the film in the United States. Since this ultimately would be the platform on which most of the international marketing for the films would be based, he wanted to see how exciting the "story about the story" was. He would look at the trailers, print ads, Web material, and whatever else was available to see if it was powerful enough to motivate moviegoers in foreign markets. We think this is an important observation. It is not enough to have a great story. You have to be able to tell a great story as well.

Probably because there are more than one hundred feature films that come out each year and their shelf lives are relatively short, movie marketing forms great parallels for understanding marketing strategies in other industries. As mentioned, at one level the industry has developed a formula that uses the results from the first weekend as a fairly accurate predictor for a film's success. Other market players—DVDs, rentals, cable rights, international distribution—consider these early results as they contemplate their level of involvement after the movie opens. Having a strong first weekend helps ensure success. Of course, that has led to lots of "gaming" of the system. It has been determined that the most fluid group of moviegoers—teenage boys—can be influenced to go see a new movie at the drop of a backward baseball cap, while other groups—middle-aged men, for example—are more likely to plan many days ahead. So, what happens is that the system can be gamed by a lousy film that is able to run a thirty-second spot on MTV that will pull teenage boys on the weekend the movie opens. Although it might sound like a sly trick, it is a big play that works.

The Land of the Living Dead

LOLD is our acronym for Land of the Living Dead—those companies that have lost all hope of ever returning value to their investors and are just "going through the motions" of being a start-up company. The way that companies end up in LOLD varies—some did not get their products just right, others did not execute on the sales side, some never had their business models right in the first place. Whatever the reasons, they have ended up in a valley from which they are unable (or unwilling) to escape. They still plod along—maybe because, despite their ineptness, they are still able to get a few customers who provide them with a meager revenue stream, or maybe they still have several million in the bank left over from a previous round of funding. Whatever the reason, the one thing that these companies have in common is that they are time wasters. Whenever we run into one of them we try to get them out of our offices as soon as we can; we have better ways to use our time than to hear their stories.

A common wisdom across the LOLD companies is that somehow they have come to believe that "just getting by" is OK. We often hear them say something like, "We'll soon be cash flow positive," as if that was an oasis that would provide refuge from the cruel business world that they are operating in. Being cash flow positive without significant growth simply means that you are running a small business—the dress shop on the ground floor of our building may be cash flow positive but it is not something to write home about. If it was your uncle's candy store they were talking about, being cash flow positive would be pretty important since it probably meant there was more money coming into the till than going out, and he would have enough to support his family. But that is not what we are talking about here. Investors in an innovative company do not gain anything when the company cannot pull off a substantial liquidity event. To do that they need a big idea that eventually will translate into a significant jump in valuation. Investors, in fact, are probably losing a lot of money by staying involved with a company that does not understand its big picture and the size of its market opportunity. They are just losing time, and, as they say, *time* is *money*. In an important market segment, when a company runs out of steam and is just limping along, time actually becomes more valuable than money. If the segment is important, then good ideas will be funded and investors will have a chance to make serious money. A company that has pared itself to the break-even level too often has jettisoned most of its development staff and, consequently, has put itself in a position where it cannot outperform its competitors. They have long since past the point where their time is worth more than the money the company will generate.

Investors make money only when they have really big successes. Although having companies in their portfolio that are scratching to reach the point of only being cash flow positive without having the prospects of capitalizing on an important market opportunity may make for nice conversation at the nineteenth hole, a LOLD company takes investors' valuable time away from finding and nurturing big successes. Because smart investors have better things to do, they walk away from companies that have lost track of their big ideas. Suppose you were a venture investor with a $250 million fund spread over twenty-five companies, and one of your portfolio companies showed you a plan that was essentially aimed at breaking even over a three-year period, without any significant growth. Would you (a) cheer them on, or (b) shut them down so that you could at least recapture a fraction of your original investment and allow yourself to reallocate the four or five weeks each year that managing this investment would have taken?

A troubled company, positive cash flow status notwithstanding, should first and foremost be looking for the big play if it wants to remain in the game. If it does not, it will suffer a fate worse than shutting down by drawing in a weak set of investors. (Remember, we are saying that there is still far too much venture investment available to everyone so it is not only the "A" teams that will continue to get investments.) Pity the investors who have nothing better to do with their time than to enjoy the busywork created by a LOLD company that spends its next three years working a weak business plan into the ground. The difficulty is worsened by the fact that this is a slow death; each month the company loses ground to competitors that are executing their big plays. Eventually, management and investors alike should realize that having a company in the sector that is scraping by at breakeven is not working out. The competition has outdistanced them, and they have essentially run out of options.

BIG ENERGY

While our criteria for the big idea may seem too simple, it is important to operate at this level for the very simple reason that innovative products and services need big play strategies to win. You must anticipate the bigness of what you are doing in advance, while there are still sufficient time and resources to make course corrections to improve your own bigness factors.

Whether it is the next greatest disk drive or a new medical device, it seems that the bigger the idea, the bigger the changes that are going on in the market. It is only natural that spending increases during times when things are changing in markets. In the 1990s, when decentralization and departmental computing were in vogue, companies spent billions to acquire the technologies needed to support these systems. In today's markets when the opposite is going on and centralization is sought, companies are again spending large sums to reach these goals.

Changes are going on in markets all the time. The best big plays that we have seen are the ones that tap into these naturally occurring changes and use them as energy sources to propel the big play. A simple surfing metaphor works well. You have a surfboard and want to use it. You would not take your board to a beach on a small lake because there are no significant waves there. You go to an ocean beach that has huge waves. The bigger the better. You do this because surfing involves successfully tapping into the energy of the wave so that you can ride its crest. Simple idea. Straightforward plan. You go to the ocean because that is where the energy is.

So too with the big play. Your job is to define your big play as the method in by which you transfer energy from the market to suit your own business purpose. Find what is changing in the market, tap into it, and make it work for you.

So where do Expert Interviews we talk so much about come into this? You already know the answer. To develop ideas for big plays, your job is to determine now what the big changes are on the horizon. What is going to be changing just as your innovation enters the market? Do you have the right surfboard to ride the big wave? To determine that, you are going to lock into the future. And Expert Interviews are the way to find out today what is going to be changing tomorrow.

Chapter 6

Finding the Future

Those who can't remember the past are condemned to repeat it.
—George Santayana

Paying Attention

It is more than amazing that so many companies destroy their already limited chances for success because they understand little about their market and their competition. A good marketer spins his story as if his company is unique—that is the job and we expect it. But there is no excuse for being ignorant of the actual market or the competition. Many companies say something like "we're making stuff for branch offices to use," and when we ask how many branch offices there are in, say, the United States, the marketers do not seem to have a clue (by the way, the answer is that there are about 1.3 million branch offices, depending on how you count them). And, better yet, we've lost count of the times that companies tell us who their competitors are and leave out the really big ones, like Microsoft. And, when we ask, they'll say something like; "Golly, customers don't like them." It is one thing to be ignorant of the market history, but it's quite another thing to not understand the present market conditions, including competitors, and to not have a fact based prediction of what the future will be like. Many marketers want to think that there had been total vacuum in their space before their company came on the scene. That is their egos talking and is usually far from the truth. Wanting to believe that you are the first to arrive is not a good excuse for not knowing about what is going on right now—especially when competitors are working hard at letting people know what *they* plan to do. For software companies our favorite question is: "Can you tell us again how you're going to beat Microsoft in this market?" Truthful statements presented in a nominally honest matter may lead otherwise reasonable people to creatively reach wrong conclusions. But there is no excuse for being ignorant of either history or competition. As philosopher George Santayana once famously observed: "Those who cannot remember the past are condemned to repeat it." Ask the right questions; do not just accept the conventional wisdom. Do your homework and the future will be easier to glimpse. Successful entrepreneurs have always learned from the mistakes of their predecessors in order to avoid making them a second (or third) time. This is the most important research you can do. The right strategy will inevitably follow.

Treating Microsoft Seriously

Part of getting it right is knowing when the light at the end of the tunnel really is a freight train heading your way. We are continually amazed at the testosterone lemming instinct that has young male entrepreneurs bent on beating Microsoft (or Cisco, Intel, pick your favorite 900-pound gorilla). Microsoft in 2004 spent $6.5B on R&D, and they have shown repeatedly that once they understand a problem, they keep plugging away and ultimately get it right enough to smoke the competition (as was the case with Novell, Sun, Apple, Netscape, to name just a few). The truth is that you *can* compete with these giants, but you have to use the jujitsu technique of using their own weight against them (i.e., do something they chose not to do for their sensible business reasons). If you think you can beat them in a fair fight then you will discover what it feels like to have 900 pounds sitting on your chest. Netscape is a great example. Netscape clearly understood the Internet long before Bill Gates did, and in that time, if Bill did not get it then you could assume Microsoft would not get it either. Eventually Gates (and then Microsoft) did get it but by that time Netscape had a nice $300M/year business going and felt wonderfully smug about how they were kicking Redmond's butt. (To be sure, Microsoft creates enough animosity to assure a crowd of sycophant supporters to egg you on if you have wounded them at all.) A business magazine writer, the story goes, had once gotten all pumped up talking to Marc Andreessen in Mountain View and headed up to talk to Steve Ballmer in Redmond to watch him writhe in pain as Netscape's assured victory was presented. The reporter asked Ballmer what he was going to do to deal with Netscape. Ballmer paused thoughtfully and took a moment to admit freely that Microsoft's Internet understanding had been a long time coming. But then he faced the reporter, looked him right in the eye, and said that what he was going to do to deal with Netscape was to invest an additional $1B/ year in R&D aimed at the Internet—that was what he was going to do. Although $1B was a big deal in late 1990s for all but a few, it was clear this was not a hollow threat. It was entirely within Ballmer's capabilities to do just that (and he did). His last comment to the reporter was that he should go back and ask Netscape what *they* planned to do about Microsoft's incremental $1B R&D investment, knowing full well that Netscape was already spending a hefty $50M (1/20th of what Microsoft was spending) of their $300M in revenues on R&D, so they did not have many options that were going to sound very good, unless you assumed that Microsoft was just plain stupid, and there is more than enough evidence that was not the case. Netscape ignored the challenge and the rest is history.

You would think with all of these companies getting mowed down by Microsoft that high-tech entrepreneurs would learn how to avoid them. Today, Microsoft is spending something well north of $1B on incremental investment to improve the security of the Windows platform, and yet Silicon Valley is full of bright male and female lemming eyes running security companies that are betting that Microsoft is stupid. It is a poor bet. You cannot get it right if the train hits you.

DIRECTED DISCUSSIONS

Great business decisions require great anticipation, or luck, or a combination of the two. Being able to anticipate the future helps shift the odds in your favor. Through our work in this area, we have developed some simple techniques that help draw out discussions about where the future is heading. These directed discussions are actually useful instruments that we use to help drive discussions of what is about to happen and why. They have a common element: They do not look directly at the success; instead they are looking for the results of the success (kind of like the way that you watch an eclipse of the sun by not looking directly at the sun but instead watching the effects). Each is useful for driving a discussion with someone involved with the area you are investigating. They describe simple, straightforward ways to anticipate the future that initially draws on knowledge that you and others may already have about the business you are in. And finally, the reason that we like directed discussions so much is that they inspire hypotheses that we can investigate by finding experts to speak with.

BACK FROM THE FUTURE—WRITE NEXT YEAR'S ANNUAL REPORT TODAY

Corporate annual reports are an interesting category of literature, chronicling the life of a corporation as it evolves year in and year out. Most annual reports provide a retrospective of what occurred during the past twelve to eighteen months and an anticipation of what is in store for the future. More specifically, the president's letter is generally a two- or three-page synopsis of what occurred and how the company plans to make the most uses of its resources to generate future profits.

We have found that the structure of an annual report and its president's letter works as a useful vehicle for asking people to summarize the business results that can occur from a successful technology venture. We often use a question in the form: "Imagine if everything you're planning to do works out and that we're a couple of years in the future writing the annual report summarizing a very successful year. Then what are some of the highlights that we'd include in this report—which customers are using the products, how did it add value, in what segments, who are the business partners, what are the most important channels?"

The idea of writing tomorrow's annual report today is a simple exercise. It puts you in the position of projecting yourself into a room eighteen months from today and preparing to write the annual report for the prior year (which, of course, has not happened). Since the general formats of annual reports are well understood, this exercise forces you to consider what are the most important events that can occur—those that will have significant impact on the valuation of the company—which customer wins, which technology differentiation, which sales channels set the foundation for important business to be transacted, and documents the successful deployment of the innovation. In other words, what were the factors that led to the success? The goal of this exercise is to crisply express the higher order factors for success, all within the confines of an hour or so. The value in doing this, of course, is that it helps clarify your thinking regarding which goals are the most important to achieve.

IMMERSION

A variation of writing the annual report for your business is to take the perspective of one of your future customers and address the question of how they might describe in their annual report the business benefits that come from using your innovation. Although they hardly ever do it, salespeople are taught in basic selling classes to read their customers' annual reports. The reason for doing this is your prospective customer's annual report generally talks about their technology investments—what they are doing, how much they are spending, and what value they are deriving from them. There is a good reason why this happens. In most large companies, information technology spending ranges from 2 percent to 10 percent of revenues, depending on the industry and the state of a particular company within that industry. For an investment of this size, it is only natural that the shareholders of the company are interested in how the company is deriving value from such a large investment.

So, salespeople are told, rightly, to check out the annual report because it will provide a ten thousand foot-view of a potential customer's technology investment strategy and what the most important value returns from that investment will be. Often, the key to selling an innovative new product is right there, free of charge, courtesy of your own customer's CEO. From this starting point, it is up to the salesperson to link a specific sales situation to this higher goal.

A good salesperson will develop an "elevator pitch" for each major account in the pipeline. The essence of the pitch is to imagine that you have the undivided attention of the CEO of your potential customer for only a few seconds. What would you say? Our proposal is that, having complete knowledge of what the CEO is telling shareholders about his rationale for their IT investment (because you have read the annual reports), then you are in a position to make the case as to how and why what you do helps achieve his goals. The point of developing this sort of "elevator" message is that the salesperson is not the only one who has to synthesize the buying justification down to a few simple statements; the customer's own team must eventually do so in order to get internal funding, and a great elevator pitch works wonders for them as well.

Many people are turned off by this type of reasoning because they think their products are such a small piece of the picture that doing this really does not make much sense. If you are one of those, then just skip to the next section because you are not going to like what follows. Our experience is the opposite. A customer's annual report, especially the president's letter to the shareholders, often points to the exact value proposition that is most important—maybe quality improvements are of major concern, or improving customer service, or simplifying their customers' experiences. Since that is the case, then how will your customer describe the inclusion of your innovation in its annual summary?

Of course in an innovative new category, you are considering a somewhat longer term view of the situation. So, as a discussion exercise, considering the way that your customers will eventually justify to their shareholders the investment that they will be making in your innovation will be very useful. Maybe it is just a sentence or a paragraph in a future letter from the CEO to shareholders. What is important is to get into the mindset of your customer's top executive as he or she might talk to shareholders about the potential business value that your innovation holds. Although it is a simple statement, it is a powerful thought if you can get to it. Too often, innovators do not have enough "touch and feel" for the situations they are looking into, and our immersion process is a way to develop an important additional strategic perspective.

I'll take Door #3, Monty

It is an interesting fact of probability that on *Let's Make a Deal*, you would have improved your odds by always choosing the other door when the show's host Monty Hall gave you the chance to switch. The right choice in the high-tech world is to bet against schemes based on difficult engineering. Someone can always invent and build a product like the Segway, but never ask if the concept made enough business sense to justify the effort. Despite grandiose claims that their invention would "change the way cities are built," the engineers and investors behind Segway never came up with the "killer app." At the introduction, the Segway team talked about how the U.S. Postal Service was seriously evaluating Segway and would soon be placing large orders. Walking turns out to be a pretty good alternative for most of us, and allows good access as well. Although Segway's engineering is fascinating and the business story behind its invention is the stuff that movies are made about, the part they could not explain was why there was a market for what they were building. It was one of those conversations that we hear all too often: Prospective customer: "Why do I need one?" Innovator: "Look how fast it goes!" Prospective customer: "How does that help me run my business so much better that I'll pay your price?" Innovator: "You can't go anywhere near this fast!" Prospective customer: "Yes, but walking seems to have worked quite well, I think I'll wait, but thank you very much." If they had taken any time to look at the market, Segway's results would have been much better. As of this writing, a wheelchair based on the Segway technology has been introduced. This is probably the product that they should have come out with first. Let us hope that they are able to survive their initial disappointment to find out what's behind door number 2.

POSTER BOY MARKETING

Another in this series of anticipatory projections is something we call "poster boy marketing." This refers to determining what customer best exemplifies the use of an innovative product in a way that "everyone gets" and makes this company the "poster boy." Again, by thinking this through early in the process, and then working back from the poster boy, you can gain a clear focus on the elements of your strategy that are most important and learn about the ones that have to be overcome in order for you to succeed.

Traditionally, innovative companies have used reference accounts to improve credibility in front of prospective customers. The idea, of course, is to show potential new customers that they are not the first; other customers have successfully gone done the path before them. Poster boy marketing takes the idea of reference accounts to a new level by picking a company that is visionary in its use of your new technology and functions superbly as *the* model. If they work with you (and you would not have picked them to be your poster child if they had not), they will be invaluable in demonstrating uses of your application in such a strong way that others in the similar situations will flock to your standard. In a sense, the poster boy serves as a communicator so that many others will quickly understand the power of your innovation. Even though the technology may be quite complex, its use by the poster boy will be accomplished in a way that everyone—potential customers, channel partners, and even investors—can understand. Something that was complicated is made simple, and the poster boy provides the example.

The same type of poster boy thought process can be applied to picking the "perfect" channel and best business partners. If your idea is as good as you say it is, you will be expected to deliver it to new customers with what they consider to be "top-tier" relationships.

The quality of your poster boy, initial distributors, and strategic business partners makes a great deal of difference to prospective new customers. We cannot begin to count the number of times that companies tell us about their exciting new products (of which we are naturally skeptical) and then tell us that their first customer is some really obscure company that is not really in their target market. We've recently had a company tell us that their big reference customer was the second largest school district in Norway—could they possible have picked an organization that is more obscure? Look, if you are saying that what you do improves manufacturing, then show us that General Motors is one of your first customers. If you want to sell a golf ball that travels far, you will sign up Tiger Woods. If you are selling Viagra to older men, you get Bob Dole. If you are selling the next great product for financial services companies, you need to show us Merrill Lynch, the New York Stock Exchange, or CitiBank as customers, and not some wimpy company that your brother-in-law works for.

KILLER VALUE PROPOSITIONS—MAKING AN OFFER THAT THEY CAN'T REFUSE

Getting the value proposition right is one of the biggest factors that can affect the success or failure of an innovative company. Too often, people wait until their new products are about to come off the production line before they really focus on understanding their true value proposition. The sad fact is that there are not many value propositions to choose from in the first place, and, within a category, most of your competitors will flock to the same ones. Since everyone is going to end up at more or less the same point with the same general value proposition, your job becomes figuring out how to express the value propositions in ways that are powerfully motivating. To lift an idea from *The Godfather*, make them an offer that they can't refuse.

Turning an average value proposition into a highly charged motivation is something that sounds like common sense, but again for reasons that we do not quite understand, it is rare when we see this actually happen. In fact, we generally see the opposite when companies express their value propositions in a general framework, leaving it up to their customers to figure out whether it is going to be worth all the effort that will be required to make a change.

And then there are the return on investment (ROI) value propositions. While the concept of ROI as a value proposition is pretty straightforward ("buy this product, and here is the improvement to your bottom line"), they generally fail to create differentiation from one vendor to another. There are a lot of reasons why we say this, not the least of which is that the "old" way of doing something is generally so cost-inefficient that when a new category emerges, the savings distinctions from one vendor to another are often overshadowed and provide little in the way of distinction.

Take "utility computing" for example. If you have not heard by now, utility computing is the current rage of computer hardware and software vendors making a point of having users operate their systems as if they were, heaven help us, power utilities. The points that these vendors are trying to make are in the vein of simplifying the operational aspects of running their data centers through system consolidation and ultimately standardization. They believe that, in the end, they can improve the system availability and decrease costs. The negative about this is, of course, that if the end point is really utility computing, then it is really hard to distinguish one vendor's utility computer operation from another vendor's system. To carry the power utility metaphor to another degree, it is really hard for their customers to know whether they are getting their power from a Con Edison fossil fuel generator in New York or from the Tennessee Valley Authority's water driven generation system. Not only can you not tell, but it is not really important, as long as the power comes when you need it. You end up not with a distinct "brand" that everyone must have, but a commodity. The savings that one vendor offers a customer with their utility computing vision compared to another vendor's system is not really due to the specific vendor's attributes as much as to the fact that the customer is changing their operational aspects of their data center by eliminating complexity and adopting a more efficient approach.

So our suggestion is that these vendors downgrade the "utility" aspects of a system, and the consequential ROI story, and instead head toward "killer value propositions" that pack a real punch. For example, what if these vendors look at the overall competitive nature of the customer's industry. As mentioned earlier, most major corporations are spending between 2 percent and 10 percent of their revenues on information technology. Of that, the operational aspects of their IT organization are often on the order of 60 percent, with the remaining spending split equally with maintenance and new initiatives, each getting about 20 percent. The affect that utility computing may have on these economics is to reduce operational spending to 40 percent, while increasing the new initiative spending to 40 percent—that means doubling the budgets for new application deployment—something that is surely to help a customer become more competitive in their industry. Well, if that is the case, then this turns out to mean that a given customer would be able to double the rate at which they bring new apps online. This becomes a killer value proposition for a vendor, because it demonstrates that not all utility computing vendors are the same. Just being able to provide utility components is not enough if you cannot also provide the ability to double the rate at which customers can bring new apps online.

As we have said, we are amazed at how little work goes into figuring out value propositions, and value propositions are too often pasted onto a product after it has been built. What if this process was reversed and the killer value propositions were established before the product's design was complete? Sounds simple enough. The results might be a dramatically improved product that continuously surprises as customers derive value from it.

Total Cost of Ownership—Distinctions without Differences

Out of our work as analysts we see lots and lots of companies coming through with the exact same cost savings value propositions that, almost always, are purely fiction. Despite the fact that vendors invest hundreds of hours promoting cost savings, they are really doing themselves a disservice because they are not building a case for their own unique, differentiated value. Selling cost savings creates problems at several levels. Sellers claiming savings as their primary value proposition are fundamentally limiting the valuations of their own companies because, at the end of the day, the value they provide to customers will never be greater than the net of the potential savings minus the transition costs. In other words, if you are selling something that saves someone one hundred dollars and it costs ten dollars to switch, then at the most, what you are selling will be worth no more than ninety dollars, and, most likely, you will only be able to charge a portion of that amount. Another big problem that we have with companies that promote cost savings as their leading value proposition is that, most often, the savings that they are talking about come directly to the customer from taking action to initiate a change; it is not something that comes from the particular attributes of a product. It is like painting a house. Yes, there is a definite ROI that comes from painting your house, and the cost of painting is less than the return that comes from both a higher resale value as well as lowered maintenance costs. But that is true no matter which painter or brand of paint you use. While there may be slight differences that derive from the various alternatives, the big payoff of an increased resale value overwhelms the differences. Our advice—demote the ROI-based value propositions to the bottom of your list of value propositions in order to allow you to develop higher order value propositions improving your customers' sales, market share, customer retention—all of these can help you express to customers your unique differentiation. We are not saying don't make ROI claims. We are saying develop strong value propositions in addition to your ROI claims.

KILLER APP

Ever since Larry Downes coined the term "killer app" in his book *Unleashing the Killer App: Digital Strategies for Market Dominance*, it has become a useful way to describe the demand impact that an innovation can have when it truly strikes a chord with customers. A killer application is technology that makes such a big difference customers are immediately attracted to it for the substantial benefits they will derive from it. It is such an important concept that we use it frequently when we are talking to experts about a potentially important innovation—questions like "Do you think that this is a killer app?" or when we are talking to a vendor bringing a new product to market, we will ask, "Can you tell us what's the killer app for your product?"

Conversely, when we talk to many executives about their new products and ask questions to the effect of, "What's the killer application that's going to drive demand for your product?" we are often met with a blank stare. It happens so often that we have gotten used to the reaction. The idea of a killer application is such a simple, straightforward concept but many companies fail to link their innovations to clear-cut killer applications that can drive their demand. The companies that do have a killer app in sight are more than happy to answer these questions and actually draft off the slipstream created by killer app demand. Others, who have not created a clear connection between what they do and a killer app, do not want to even discuss the idea. The wonderful thing about the idea of a killer app is the enormous simplification that comes with it. By being able to describe your innovation in terms of a larger kill app that it is associated with, you get to drop the "geek speak," which only a few experts comprehend, and instead talk in terms that most of us understand—improving a well-known application.

In terms of anticipating the future, the idea following the "trail" of a killer application greatly simplifies the task of trying to predict the future. You can simplify the task of understanding a variety of diverse innovations by following the killer applications within a specific industry—those applications that appear to have the most to offer to that industry. In today's economy, some examples are: radio frequency identification (RFID) in the retail industry, which holds great promise for compressing the supply chain; IT Service Management (ITSM) in the information technology management market, which can make a tremendous difference in improving system availability; and straight through processing (STP) in the financial services industry, which reduces the time needed to clear securities transactions. Rather than trying to understand the future of a specific innovation, a better way to look at the future would be to instead find the larger, more visible killer app to analyze.

And, if you are one of those who does not have a ready answer to our "what's your killer app?" question, maybe it is time to go and seek one out. Instead of saying something like "Well, we just don't have a killer app here but we've sure got an innovative new product," maybe it is time to go out and find a killer app that you can link up with. Being part of an ecosystem that is boosted by the adoption of a killer app is a pretty good thing. Remember: Not being part of killer app is not a good thing; that is a problem you will need to correct. If you do not have a killer app that you are part of, then our advice to you is: Go find one.

CO-OPTING CHAOS

As a pioneer in building strategic healthcare businesses, Lance Piccolo, former CEO of Caremark, puts it: "In chaos there is opportunity." Chaos means that things are probably changing. And, as we have said earlier, change provides energy to the market, which, ultimately, can be a very good thing. So if you are trying to predict the future, then it is reasonable to look for chaotic conditions. Probably the best recent example of a company that successfully exploited chaotic market conditions is Canada-based Research in Motion (RIM), producers of the popular Blackberry mobile e-mail system. To many, e-mail appears to be a relatively simple and friendly application. But when you look under the covers, you realize that it is one of the most complicated applications in the world—more people use e-mail than even Web browsers, people spend more time in front of e-mail screens than any other application, and e-mail interconnects almost all computer systems that have been or will be produced. In other words, e-mail is both massive and pervasive.

When RIM first started to design its Blackberry device, the world of mobile e-mail systems was totally chaotic. Wireless networks were in flux as operators were in the process of converting their networks from analog to digital, and there was a variety of standards competing for dominance. Wireless coverage was an issue. The handheld device category was awash with competing products, each with different form factors with little or no built-in wireless networking, forcing users wanting connectivity to add external wireless support, which had the unfortunate effect of depleting already short battery life. And the popular e-mail systems from Microsoft and IBM/Lotus, which were used by most businesses, had no effective mobility options. So RIM was entering a market that was completely in flux.

And this chaos turned out to be just what the doctor ordered. RIM decided to take care of all of these problems by starting with a simple design point—give the customer just one decision to make if they wanted to have mobile e-mail (buy their Blackberry device), and RIM would take care of all the rest. To take care of the problem of getting the form factor right, RIM developed its own device, complete with a functional keyboard, enough display area to read e-mail and a well-engineered battery management scheme that kept it working on a single charge for such an incredibly long time that it felt like it had a miniature nuclear reactor inside. RIM took care of the wireless networking problems by organizing its own nationwide wireless network (arguably not the most advanced wireless network of its time but, due to the nature of e-mail, this fact did not really matter to customers since it was more than good enough for moving e-mail around) and sold its wireless service under a simple rate plan for users for a fixed monthly price (no roaming charges or utilization premiums). And finally, RIM solved the problem of getting e-mail from corporate servers by providing the integration software necessary to redirect e-mail onto their network.

So by organizing what previously was completely chaotic, what RIM did was nothing less than amazing. Rather than having to make a bunch of complicated choices, their customers just had to make one, and it was a well-reasoned alternative at that. The only question that RIM had for its corporate customers was: "How many do you want?"

Our main point? Chaos, if you can find it, can be good, especially if you can tame it. If you are interviewing experts and they start telling you about how unsettled things are, that is good news and is certainly worth exploring further. Finding out just how fluid market conditions are, what the drivers are behind this, determining whether the chaos will dissipate on its own, and what the ultimate stability conditions may turn out to be can put you on the right path. When you are looking into the future, chaos is something that you should seek out. And if you can find it, you will be happy that you did.

WHAT'S THE BUSINESS MODEL?

When markets are disrupted there is often an opportunity to change the business model. When that opportunity exists, those who take advantage of it often walk away with the largest rewards. But all too often, management teams never consider these options, and their innovations enter the market using business models inherited from the very products they were planning to disrupt, and they miss a big opportunity.

Many years ago we ran into an entrepreneur who had made a fortune cleaning disk drives for a living. Disk drives actually cost thousands of dollars then and were not today's nearly disposable commoditized technology by any means. The entrepreneur had made a small fortune by buying disk drives (at ten cents on the dollar) that had failed the manufacturer's final quality control tests, opening them up, cleaning the disk platter with a special solvent, retesting them, and then selling them back to the manufacturer as fully functional new products—at five times the price he paid for them. This was a good deal for both sides since he made money and the drive manufacturers got working new drives at less than their manufacturing costs. He never told the drive manufacturers about his little trick; instead, he had them thinking that his quality teams spent hours adjusting and tweaking each drive. Little did they know that his successful business was entirely based on simple deficiencies in their platter manufacturing process. When we asked him why he did not just sell the solvent to the drive manufacturer, he said, "You must be crazy—I'd sell them maybe a drum of the solvent every three or four years, and I would hardly make any money on it." It is a simple story with a valuable lesson. Being innovative and getting it right the first time is not limited to innovation in just technology or marketing. Find a business model that lets you maximize your ability to leverage the opportunity.

Sometimes the issue is that the business model used does not match well with the value proposition being offered and actually limits the success of the idea. We see products whose value proposition is that the product is much simpler to operate and administer than what is on the market, only to see that the product is priced far greater than the customer savings from the improvements. The price does not match the value proposition.

The Internet and the investment land rush ushered in business model changes across a whole set of industries. With investment money easy to get, companies rushed free products to the market with hope of making up for lost revenues with an even more attractive upgrade offering downstream for real money. Netscape was perhaps the most innovative user of this concept, but there were, and are, many others. Products ranging from e-mail clients (Eudora, whose commercial e-mail client product was marketed by Qualcomm) to Tripwire (a commercial version of a freely downloaded application that alerts administrators when server software has changed) have come into the market through the idea of "give them a free version and then sell them the better version."

Real market disruption often has a broad impact through the market. The business model is an important part of innovation and is worth some serious out-of-the-box thinking.

Chapter 7

Positioning for Change

Plurality should not be posited without necessity. (Otherwise stated: the simplest answer is usually the right one.)

— Occam's Razor

Positioning Is Everything

Several years ago Oracle asked us to help with their positioning. At the time, the Internet was beginning to take off like a missile, and Oracle was not satisfied with its strategy. Despite the fact that Oracle had created a separate Internet division, they felt they were being left in the dust as the rest of the world moved ahead. Much attention had been paid to new Internet software development tools and application servers—the products that were produced by a number of high profile Internet software companies. So it was only natural for Oracle's marketing team to build its positioning around the latest releases of their own developer tools, which had recently been upgraded with some new Internet functionality. The trouble was that their positioning was having little effect and was not propelling the company into any significant new markets.

We interviewed about 120 experts across many different Oracle constituencies, including customers of their developer tools, customers in their best markets, competitors, competitor reference accounts, sales reps in major markets, and systems integrators. Early in the process we realized why they were having problems with their positioning—their Internet development tool was not very good compared to the application development tools that were currently popular. The primary reason why Oracle's application development tool was having problems in the market was not because of software bugs; it was just that a developer tool for a database was quite a bit different than a general purpose Internet development toolset. Oracle's product had not been designed to compete with these other products. Wanting to compete in the sexy Internet development tool market, Oracle had taken the first available tool it came across, dressed it up with the appropriate Internet terminology, and pressed it into battle.

Finding out how to solve this problem was another matter. The deeper we probed, the more elusive the answer became. The further down the development tool path we went, the more it seemed that the business of Internet development tool middleware was not at that time on Oracle's agenda—its heart still being in the database development business. There were several consistent things that kept coming up from the interviews that we were doing with customers across different market segments: the Internet was important; for building their new Internet applications customers would require databases that were both broader (each record would contain more fields) and deeper (there would be more records); and that most customers were using at least one Oracle database. So if you were building an e-Business site, it was likely that you would need a bigger, faster database than you would have used on prior applications and because you were expecting a lot of use of the new service, there were more things that you had to track. And since it may in fact be directly serving your customers, it would have to be very fast or your own brand might suffer. While any single interview did not answer our question as to what Oracle's positioning should be, taken as a group they formed a consistent message—the generation of Internet applications that were being built were going to require big and fast databases, something that Oracle knew a lot about.

Another finding related to how the market already was familiar with Oracle. There are often several databases that are part of a complex application, and often these customers used databases from several vendors. Most used Oracle in conjunction with a competitive product from either IBM or Microsoft. When we compiled our interviews, we realized that about two-thirds of the companies that we spoke with used Oracle, 40 percent used IBM, and about 20 percent used Microsoft. Rather than showing Oracle's market position as a bar chart where the total percentages owned would be more than 100 percent due to the fact that many customers used databases from more than one vendor, we chose to use a pie chart to show Oracle's market share. This created a wonderful image showing two-thirds of the pie as Oracle users.

We were at the point where we knew the answer—Internet applications were the fastest-growing new area in high tech, the databases that were required for these applications would be bigger (and more expensive) than what companies already were using, and that Oracle was the incumbent. So why not declare Oracle the leader in the fastest-growing portion of the database market with the most lucrative potential? Shown as a pie chart, across the industries that we had interviewed, two out of every three users were Oracle users; this image created a very powerful message. This pie chart became the enduring symbol of Oracle's new positioning campaign—Oracle drives the Internet.

As part of the ongoing positioning campaign, we chased down specific market segments—overall Fortune 100, the top e-commerce sites, the top Christmas retailers—and the same story revealed itself. Each of these segments had new Internet-based applications under construction, requiring bigger and faster databases, and the majority used Oracle. Oracle's positioning was extended to each important market segment under the same banner—Oracle's database drives the underlying functionality for the majority of users in each of these segments. Rather than having a "me too" positioning as they tried with their development tool positioning, Oracle's new positioning moved the company to the position of thought leadership in the emerging category of Internet e-business application development. It was not too long after this that Oracle was considered a best practices solution to high-end Internet application development. As for Oracle's developer tools, the original positioning that Oracle had used, sales for these products shot up as well, since new customers choosing to use Oracle's databases were inclined to buy their developer tools as part of their development configuration.

Positioning as a "Systems Company"

For decades, positioning consultants have told their clients that they have to "act like a systems company." The idea was that you if you positioned yourself as the supplier of a complex system (instead of simply selling a component), you could greatly increase the value you delivered to your customer. Whether you made computers, sophisticated laser systems, or complex medical devices, being a systems supplier meant listening closely to your customer, becoming an expert on the entire problem that they were trying to solve, and combining your products with whatever else was needed to provide a comprehensive solution.

But a lot has changed. Back in the "old days," companies were selling innovative solutions to customers who did not have very much in the way of technology—customers who were using traditional labor-intensive traditional business practices to get their jobs done. So the new systems were brought into "greenfield" situations—environments that had little or no computerization. Becoming a systems company then was a pretty good idea.

The biggest change is that today's customers are no longer operating in greenfield environments. In fact, they have become sophisticated technology buyers. Today's customers already own and operate complex systems. That puts a new spin on the concept of being a systems company. Today's innovative companies are selling to customers who operate complex systems. The "systems company" is now the buyer, not the seller. Being a systems-oriented vendor in today's markets means understanding the complexities of the major systems that your customer relies on to operate a business, and then delivering functionality that not only fits into their existing systems environments but also increases the value that these systems deliver to customers. The vendor's role is to fit into the systems their customers already own and operate.

We think that these changes in the market—having sophisticated, technology-literate customers—will have a big impact on the traditional systems company positioning and ultimately will drive suppliers to realize that it is now their customers who are the real systems companies. The supplier's job is now to first fit in and then stand out.

POSITIONING DONE RIGHT

It is easy for customers to be confused by the glut of innovative products available in today's market. Customers do not have time to learn about each and every new product in the market to decide what's right for them. Their minds are already crowded with alternatives, and yet new products keep coming into the market. That is why strategic positioning is so important. Positioning provides a vehicle for capturing share of mind among potential customers.

When done right, the positioning of a new product builds on information your customer already knows and believes. Too often companies position themselves with respect to their own belief system and not that of their customers. This is an extension of the problem created by engineers designing new products in a vacuum. Most businesspeople do not get it—the strongest positioning is developed from the ideas that are *already* in the minds of their potential customers, using words that are already in the customer's vocabulary to describe a category and create a position.

It is the sad truth of marketing in this decade that strategic positioning across highly innovative companies is significantly broken. Innovative companies have trouble establishing unique positions in the eyes of their potential customers. Positioning is muddled or, worse yet, not believable. There are many reasons for how this has come about, which we will not go into here. Suffice it to say that the turmoil from what has transpired in the past continues to cast its shadow as today's firms try to gain marketing traction.

There are three key elements for positioning done right:

1. Positioning is about the future—it takes a long time to position your company effectively so that its position is firmly established in your customers' minds. That means that effective positioning is not about what you want to be today but what you want to be in the future (go to where the puck is heading!!!).

2. Positioning works when you position yourself with respect to what customers already believe—most likely, you do not have enough money to create new categories in your potential customers' minds. In today's mass media market, even if you had the money, you are more likely to fail than succeed at doing this anyway. You must build your position on your customers' existing belief system.

3. Positioning works when your own workforce believes it—great positioning starts at home. You have to first convince your own employees about your positioning, starting with your sales force—the most effective positioning messages are delivered person-to-person. Personal contact is a great way to

show your customers what you are trying to achieve and what position you would like to occupy. But your entire company—especially all of the customer touchpoints like sales and support—needs to be in step with your positioning aspirations to carry these directly to your customer base. Developing an effective position with your customers happens best when your own workforce believes it. If your own people do not "get it," rest assured, your customers never will.

But Can It Fit in My Pocket?

The mistakes that Apple Computer made with its Newton products are a classic example of positioning done wrong. When the Newton was introduced in 1993, Apple was the center of the personal computer universe—everything was going well for the company. Apple positioned the Newton as a PDA and spent millions in advertising and promotion to get people to try it. The trouble was consumers did not really know what a PDA was. They knew what a computer was—something with a screen, keyboard, processor, and disk—and they knew that the Newton was not a computer. It was technically elegant, about the size of a large paperback book, but it did not have a killer application that made it exceptional. Consumers were never really sure what the Newton was. While the idea of a PDA perhaps made a lot of sense to the Apple people at corporate headquarters in Cupertino, the concept was a flop on Main Street. PDA was not in the consumer vocabulary yet, and to get it there it would have taken a lot more advertising and promotion dollars than Apple had to spend.

Palm Inc., on the other hand, got it right. Originally starting life as a software developer for Newton-type devices, Palm got frustrated when companies like Apple failed to gain acceptance for these types of products. So, the people at Palm decided to build its own product. They positioned their product as an "organizer." That was a brilliant move. Organizing calendar and contact information was their killer app. People knew what organizers were. The most important thing that consumers knew about this category was that an organizer must fit into a shirt pocket, which was the starting point to Palm's unique design.

THE POWER TO BE WHAT YOU WANT TO BE

For twenty years the U.S. Army used "Be All You Can Be" as its advertising slogan. We are going to steal that phrase and apply it to strategic positioning. Positioning is much more than choosing a vehicle to drive your marketing messages home to your customers. The much broader view is that positioning has the power to thrust an innovative business into the center of an emerging disruption taking place in your industry, and, by doing so, it allows your company to maximize its economic advantage. Positioning is about what you want to be, not what you are. Strategic positioning is not about what a company *is* but about what a company *can become*—again, it is "skating to where the puck will be." As we said, the three elements of positioning mean you should decide what you want to be, convince your workforce that you are going to do what it takes to deliver on this new positioning, and then effectively communicate your new positioning to customers using words that your customers already understand.

That sounds great but where do you start? It is a chicken and egg/ horse and cart problem. Which comes first? Do you decide to develop your position first and then test it out in the market? Or do you do that in reverse, by first talking to the market and then developing a position? Taking that first choice is critical because it means you have to pick your direction and then move from there. The alternative makes sense because ultimately markets act to select the messaging that resonates best. So what do you do first? Of course, we have an answer to this quandary about where to start. We call it market segmentation, and it is the subject of the next chapter. Basically, our answer is that you first find the market segments that have the most potential and then use these to develop the initial set of positioning ideas. Looking at just a few segments gives you the opportunity to focus on the groups that value what you do the most.

Confounding Your Bliss

Have you ever had one of those discussions with somebody in which they tell you about their business, and when they are done you do not have the slightest idea what they are trying to accomplish or how they will ever be able provide a return to their investors? We are sorry to report this, but it happens to us all the time. After one of these conversations we have to remind ourselves that we are supposed to be experts, so if we are coming away pretty confused, imagine what "Joe Public" must be thinking! Too often entrepreneurs complicate their business definitions so much that it is nearly impossible to understand under what circumstances their companies can ever succeed. We have an expression for it—"Stanfordizing the Problem"—because usually these entrepreneurs are very smart people with MBAs from prestigious universities like Stanford. They forget that the simplest answer is the best, and when you make situations really complex you end up losing sight of your goal and end up chasing your own tail. This is especially true for strategic positioning. Complex positioning concepts are the simplest generally hard for customers to accept. The simplest positioning statements are always the best.

THE PROBLEM WITH CONFERENCE ROOM POSITIONING

Great positioning does not happen overnight. Think about all the steps that you have to go through before you develop an effective new position. Even after you have gone through the process of creating your new positioning statement, you still must communicate it to your customers and their advisors. This takes lots of time and lots of money. And just communicating it is not enough—you must live up to the position that you are aspiring toward and substantiate it in your customers' eyes. You have been successful with your positioning only after your audience has accepted your message. The communications and acceptance part of this process is the really ugly part. How long this process takes varies widely depending on the industry segment and product category. But one thing you can count on is that it will take lots of time and perhaps lots of luck to make this happen.

Probably the biggest positioning mistake that companies make is that they underestimate the difficulties, expense, and time required to make positioning work. There is a human tendency to believe that everyone you are trying to reach shares your value system and that once they hear your brilliant positioning statement they are sure to "get it." We call people making this mistake "conference room positioners," because they think that, once they have their new position written on the conference room whiteboard, the hard work is generally done and they are just a press release away from having the world accept the new reality. Of course, it is much more difficult than this.

Positioning should be done around customers' desires. And the position that you develop should not only be in response to what customers want the most but it must also be based on what you do differently. You are looking for things that customers greatly desire and that you can put yourself in unique position of providing.

Stronger Is Better—What Do Peet's Coffee and Ben and Jerry's Ice Cream Have in Common?

Peet's Coffee and Ben and Jerry's Ice Cream have much in common. Of course both are successful food service chains. And both have built their businesses well beyond their store presence by having formed substantial businesses supplying their branded products to consumers through food retailers. But they share an important marketing distinction as well. Both Ben and Jerry's and Peet's Coffee are known for having the richest flavors in their categories. Both companies built their brands by having "jacked up" the flavor of their products. Peet's distinguishes itself from rival Starbucks for its strong coffee flavor. Ben and Jerry's claims to have developed its strongly flavored ice cream products because one of the founders' diminished sense of taste caused them to ratchet up the flavor of their ice cream so that even he could taste it. Both companies used their distinctive flavor positioning elements to appeal to the "power users" in their markets. Both succeeded in markets that were regarded as mature and stable, but by anticipating new demand based on shifting tastes, these companies were able to grow market share where it seemed nearly impossible.

THE INNOVATOR'S GUIDE TO POSITIONING

Great positioning is also simple positioning. When you look around at the leading consumer products and services, the ones that you know best most often have the simplest positioning messages. For Hertz their message is convenience—we are the biggest and the best and we are everywhere! Mountain Dew has come to mean "cool" not "country," successfully altering its own initial positioning strategy. For Starbucks, it is social—we are comfortable, we are clean, and you can hang out, read, and surf the Internet, meet friends or do business while you are here. For 7 Up it is uncola. These companies spend millions to drive home the simplest of all messages. Actually, these messages are simultaneously simple and complicated—simple because they boil down to a word, complicated because these messages project complex emotions onto a corporate brand. The simplicity of the message opens the door to a consumer's mind and allows the brand to connect to the more complex response. Without this door opener, consumers tend to reject these messages because they do not see how they fit in with what they already know. If consumers cannot quickly see how the product fits into their own world, they will unconsciously block the rest of the messaging that follows.

These same ideas hold true for positioning innovative new products and services as well. It is not what you think that matters but what your potential customers think. It is not your words that matter but the words that your customers use. It is not the product categories as you define them, it is the categories as your customers define them.

Since this is the case, then it is important that you use your customers' view of the world to define what you are doing. And of course, that is where our Expert Interview process comes in. It is really interesting when you are talking to experts to ask them how they would describe to someone else in their field what you are doing. What is the set of words they would use? How would they describe the category that you are in? Is this a new subcategory that you have created? How does this relate to the others in the field? What position does the leader occupy and how does this relate to your own positioning? These are all questions that your experts can address. And somewhere in their responses will be answers to your positioning questions.

This is a lot different than doing something like a focus group, where you bring in four or five positioning slogans and ask the participants to tell you what they are feeling. That sort of feedback can come much later in the process. At this point you are developing the concept itself.

To find the right positioning, you have to determine the categories your customers already accept as a reality. Who do they perceive as the leaders in those categories? Their perspectives matter most. And the best way to find this out is to ask them to describe the categories and the dominant vendors in their own words. After you describe to them what you are planning to do, ask them to describe what you just told them using their own words. That may sound a little awkward, but it is important to understand how they might, in turn, describe to a

colleague what you are doing. That is an important element of positioning: Positioning provides a simple way for both your potential
customers to understand what you do as well as helping them to tell
others about what you do.

We live in a world where we are flooded with marketing messages
from dawn to dusk. Unfortunately for those of us involved with
innovative new products and services, the messages that involve new
technologies compete side by side with everything else for a chance to
capture the attention of the people you value the most—your potential
customers. Even if you eliminated all of the nonbusiness messages and
just looked at the marketing messages directed at your customers from
within your industry, the situation still exists where there are lots and
lots of conflicting messages competing for a share of your customers'
attention. If you do not think so, go to a trade show in your field, stand
in the middle of the exposition, and look around at all of the vendors
selling their wares—each with their own unique market position. Your
customers are bombarded with marketing messages.

Add to this the fact that the way that most new technologies are
adopted is through a process where a few people learn about it in the
first place and then evangelize within their organization for trial
adoptions. In product adoption's simplest form, there is someone in an
organization who is tasked with fixing a problem. That person spends
a reasonable amount of time looking around for a solution and finds
one that may work. Once that person reaches a conclusion as to how to
proceed, the solution must be explained to others in the company
through some sort of internal collaboration process, which may be
pretty extensive because of the number of people who have something
to do with the decision process. This sort of inside selling is what
drives most innovative new products and services in their early phases.
It is not enough to do a good job selling your product, you must create
allies on the inside who understand the value that you provide and
have the ability to sell others in their organization on the idea. (There's
that famous expression—"You never get fired for choosing IBM,"
which, at one level, speaks to the difficulty that insiders once faced
when trying to make a "non-IBM" product selection.) Effective positioning—providing the ability to describe your value to others in a
simple manner—helps your selling efforts by simplifying the task for
the insiders that have to convince their own companies that what
you're selling is the right thing to do. So the way the system works is
that you end up selling to a few key people, your allies on the inside,

who, in turn, must convince the rest of the organization that it is the right choice. This means that your product messaging and positioning must be so good that not only does it convey a strong message to the people that you meet, but it is also good enough to help your "inside sales team" convince their peers and top management.

WHAT IS IN A WORD? EVERYTHING!

Great positioning happens when you capture a word in the minds of your customers. Sometimes it is an existing word, and other times it is up to you to find a new word. The difficulties are first finding what the word is that best describes the position you want to occupy, and then capturing that word in your customer's mind.

Expert Interviews offer a great opportunity to find out which words have meaning to your customers. Doing even a handful of Expert Interviews will give you great insight into your customers' vocabulary and put you closer to the positioning ideas that you will need to use.

CREATING KILLER VALUE PROPOSITIONS

Value propositions are the vehicles by which positioning translates into the potential that your product holds for your customers. Like positioning, value propositions are about the future. Value propositions hold the promise for what your customers can gain by working with you. They are about what your customers want to become.

To create an effective value proposition, it is very important to understand how the future might evolve. That is why using our anticipation process for interpreting the future is useful. It can give you a look at the potential of a new technology and the impact it can have on customers.

A few years ago we came to the realization that there are only about a dozen categories of value propositions that innovative companies successfully use to project their value, and for most situations, only a few of them apply. At first, this sounded strange because it is easy to think that these products and services are all unique and, therefore, the resulting value propositions should be different. But after helping hundreds of clients develop markets for their new products, we finally understood that, in reality, there are just a handful of unique value propositions that work, and most situations can only use just a few.

Knowing in advance that there are only a few value propositions that will work allows you to adopt the anticipation process that we describe by directing a set of key questions about likely value propositions. Since you know in advance that there are only a dozen value propositions that may be useful, and since some of these you can exclude based on a given situation, you are then able to discuss each of the remaining value propositions during your Expert Interviews to see which ones, if any, have substance and can gain some traction. You even have the ability to do a form of rating to get an idea of how strong the potential value propositions may be in a particular situation.

OUR "AH HA": THE TWELVE VALUE PROPOSITIONS FOR INNOVATIVE PRODUCTS AND SERVICES

It may sound surprising that innovative products and services generate only twelve unique value proposition categories, but we have come to take this as a "truth." These twelve form the master set of value propositions that companies tend to use—framing subordinate value propositions.

The good news is that these value propositions span a lot of territory—from R&D through production to customer service functions. It is rare that any specific product will cover that much territory and to be able to claim all twelve value propositions associated with each function. This presents one of those uncomfortable facts of life when you are selling innovative products and services: Since there are just a handful of value propositions and since most product categories use just a few of these, most competitors in a category will be promoting similar ones. That means you have to make the most of the ones that you have and find ways of differentiating your interpretation of the value proposition from their version. Finding your value proposition is not the hard part, the hard part is making it different than the others.

THE TOP TWELVE VALUE PROPOSITIONS

1. Increase brand awareness—Improve your customer's image with its customers. For consumers, image and status are the operative words.

2. Increase sales and reduce customer churn—Help your customers sell more, improve distribution channels, increase market share. Help your customers reduce the rate at which they lose customers.

3. Improve life—Help people live longer, cure disease, improve the quality of the work environment, improve safety, save lives, reduce accidents. We will include entertainment here as well, although you can reasonably argue that this can have a category of its own.

4. Speed up time to market—Reduce new product development time, bring new products to market faster.

5. Speed up time to open up new markets—Decrease the time it takes to enter new markets.

6. Improve quality—Make measurable improvements in quality, improve manufacturing operations, simplify manufacturing complexities (and reduce the need for retooling factory operations).

7. Improve customer service—Improve communications with customers, help your customers serve their customer better.

8. Improve compliance—Improve your customer's ability to meet government regulations.

9. Improve productivity—Help make your customer's workforce more productive, improve collaboration, and get more out of investment capital and resources.

10. Improve operations—Simplify operations, including the consolidation of multiple processes, improve information transfer and streamline corporate operations, improve your customer's ability to form new partnerships, and develop closer working relationships with suppliers.

11. Increase security—Reduce the overall security risk.

12. Reduce costs—Cut expenses and other things that reduce costs.

Knowing in advance that a few of these value propositions will ultimately be the ones that you will be putting to work for your products gives you the ability to understand the market's reaction to these value propositions better during the Expert Interviewing process. You are not on a wild goose chase looking for some exotic new value proposition. Instead, you can use Expert Interviews to better understand which of these value propositions have the most to offer and how you can increase their impact. Expert Interviews let you intimately understand why your customers will value you while your engineering teams are still in the early development phases.

THE CASE AGAINST COST SAVINGS VALUE PROPOSITIONS

We put the cost savings value proposition at the end of our list for a reason. Probably the biggest mistake that innovative companies make early is that they believe cost savings is the single biggest value that they have to offer their customers and, consequently, base their entire business strategies on it. Companies that do this are heading for a disaster. We are not saying that innovative companies should not claim cost savings as a value proposition. We are saying that it probably should be the last value proposition and certainly not the one on which to base their businesses.

The first problem with leading off with cost savings is that it is not a value proposition that is unique. Most often, it is the act of making the change in the first place that creates the majority of the cost savings with variations due to specific vendor implementations. Almost all vendors in a category can and tend to make similar cost savings claims. And because of that, cost savings value propositions offer little differentiation. Imagine a situation where one vendor claims a savings of $5, another $8, and a third $10. From the customer's standpoint, the differential across these three vendors is only $5. So the company that thinks they are giving an $8 savings is really only providing $3 of differentiated value—since everyone offers a savings of at least $5.

Another problem with leading with cost savings as a value proposition is that much of the cost savings formula is often out of your hands, since the costs that you are displacing come from things that you do not control. And that means that the companies that do control these costs may react—by reducing their prices or changing their business practices in order to reduce any advantage that you may have.

Cost savings value propositions also suffer from something that we call the law of diminishing opportunities. Cost savings differs from customer to customer. Across a similar set of customers, some will have a whole lot of savings to gain while others will not have nearly as much. Usually, there is a pretty wide range. Naturally, those with the greatest savings will be most interested in what you and your competitors do and will likely move first to become customers. That of course is good news to you in the short term. But as the most lucrative customer opportunities become customers, the overall market opportunity quickly deteriorates. The remaining customers do not see as much value in cost savings because they do not have as much of a problem, and they are wondering what new functionality you might have that means more to their businesses.

Finally, when you're selling ROI, the prices that you re charging are in the denominator of the value equation—the lower your price, the higher the ROI. Ultimately, that is not where you want to be.

DETERMINING YOUR FUTURE VALUE PROPOSITION

Positioning is not about what your product does—it is about what your customers value. Once you understand what your customers value, you are in good shape to decide what position (and what word) you would like to own in your customer's mind. If you are successful, as soon as your message starts gaining traction in the market there will be a small army of competitors lining up and, unfortunately, making similar claims. So you need to move out early to stake out your position, create value in your differentiated services, and hopefully build some entry barriers along the way. As we have described, Expert Interviews can point you in the right direction well before others have figured out the opportunity.

EXTENDING POSITIONING THROUGH PARTNERSHIPS

Another positioning dimension that Expert Interviews can help you understand relates to the partnerships you will need to extend your value propositions. Because today's businesses run complex operations involving many vendors, customers benefit when vendors partner to provide more comprehensive solutions that provide greater value than if the vendors acted individually. Expert Interviews provide a great source of information regarding which partnerships are important to support your positioning. Within most markets an ecosystem exists that has become part of the value chain, and some of these participants may be helpful for substantiating your market position. Additionally, the key suppliers in a specific market often have done a lot to position themselves within the market and may provide an opportunity to establish your own position in relation to a well-known vendor's positioning. That may greatly simplify your own positioning process.

Chemical manufacturer BASF used a very effective form of positioning themselves through their partners with their famous moniker "We don't make a lot of the products you buy. We make a lot of the products you buy better." What is wonderful about this is the shear simplicity of the statement, plus the fact that they did not actually name a specific partner but used broad categories like golf balls and carpets, leaving the details to their customer's imagination.

Chapter 8

Segmentation: Finding Your Killer Application

I know that 50% of my advertising is wasted. I just don't know which half.

—John Wanamaker

There's Nothing Small about Small Business

When IBM wanted to get closer to small and mid-size businesses, they asked an important question: Could a product they called Home Page Creator, which used a template process to simplify the creation of small business Web sites, be taken to market or should it be shelved? It was not clear to them whether this product added much value to the big picture at IBM. Since the United States has over 10 million small businesses, there was no simple answer to any of their questions regarding what the market wanted. By using our anticipation process to group these businesses into a handful of homogenous segments, and then doing Expert Interviews in each segment, they were able to quickly zero in on the facts that small businesses putting up Web sites were taking their first of many steps to incorporate the Internet into their businesses, and small businesses in segments like retail had an important relationship to much larger IBM customers in that segment. IBM realized it could use this product as the entry point for working with fast-growing small businesses in traditionally strong IBM segments.

ASYMMETRIC MARKETING—THE TWENTY-FIRST CENTURY REALITY

When you step back and look at how enterprise market segments are shaping up for the future, one fact comes through loud and clear— the days of horizontal marketing of high-tech solutions across most industry segments are gone, and in their place is something that we call Asymmetric Marketing. Asymmetric Marketing is the process of marketing very deeply in a handful of segments that are most important to you while marketing thinly in the remaining ones.

Obviously, we have lifted this term from the military's theory of Asymmetric Warfare. Its military meaning varies based on whether you are trying to describe a battleground where guerrilla fighters have an unfair advantage due to their ability to outmaneuver their enemy or you are describing the overwhelming advantage that well-equipped troops have over an ill-prepared enemy.

Asymmetric Marketing has a parallel in sports as well. Before a game, coaches are always looking to take advantage of unbalanced match-ups. For instance, if they are about to play a team that is much stronger physically, a coach may choose to put his fastest players in a position to out maneuver the stronger, but slower opponents. First identifying the right match-ups and then taking advantage of them are some of the most important decisions a coach can make.

For our purpose, Asymmetric Marketing is the situation that high-tech companies face when only a handful of market segments show high interest while customers in the other market segments are uninterested. Compared to the boom years of the 1990s, this situation frustrates many. In this decade, growth in tech spending will be modest in comparison, and not all sectors will increase their high-tech spending by an equal percentage. Instead, a few markets (like financial services and the U.S. federal government) will increase high-tech spending significantly, because they see an opportunity for business improvement. Other sectors (like manufacturing) may increase high-tech spending somewhat, and still others (state government or retailing, etc.) may remain flat and at times decline.

Many high-tech companies are not paying attention to what is happening and are acting the way they have in the past by trying to sell the same products to all markets. The reality of Asymmetric Marketing means that innovators need to re-design their approaches to their most important markets. They need to do more for the segments that care the most. Customers in the markets that care the most may be willing to pay much more for a more comprehensive solution. Asymmetric Marketers develop plans to sell deeper in fewer markets rather than skimming with equal penetration across several market segments.

Of course, to get Asymmetric Marketing right, you must get your market segmentation right in the first place. We developed a modified version of our anticipation process specifically to identify market segments correctly, well in advance of actually bringing products into the market. It is our belief that following "best practices" in the new product planning process means that the market segmentation identification for a new concept should be completed in parallel with the development of the product specifications—well ahead of actually starting to build the product.

If you understand the concept of Asymmetric Marketing properly, there is good news here: There will be plenty of opportunities for growth and profit as future markets for innovative products and services develop. The bad news is that if you are not an Asymmetric Marketer, these opportunities may appear at first to be too small to notice. You will be focused on a large, foreboding universe rather than on the few planets that may support life. High-tech marketers need to take a page out of the U.S. military's playbook and reengineer their plans for the battle that they are about to fight. Or be like NASA and go to Mars, not to every planet in every constellation.

GETTING SEGMENTATION RIGHT

We have used our anticipation process more than one hundred times to develop market segmentation strategies for innovative companies. Segmentation strategies are one of the most powerful tools a business team has for developing its strategic plans, yet they are often overlooked and ignored as part of the planning process. Many business strategies for innovative companies fail because they are too generic; these plans go through the motions of trying to map out a business strategy but they never get into the real issues of capturing market share. Segmentation strategies come from the opposite direction because, by their very nature, they are based on market realities within important market segments.

What Is a Market Segment?

What makes up a market segment? That sounds like a simple enough question, but it is one that can get you wrapped around your axle if you do not get it right before you begin the process. We have learned to define a market segment as a grouping of a homogenous set of customers, a grouping where the customers share some sort of value set and are likely to place a similar weight on the value they will get by investing in innovative applications. So if you were introducing a new online calendar, you might not want to lump "professionals" in the same category because some professionals, like college professors, are somewhat casual about their calendars beyond the classroom setting, while others, like doctors, are completely activity-driven by their calendars, and still others, like lawyers, have a direct legally binding relationship with their calendar (court appearances) and even use the word docket in place of calendar. So if you were trying to segment the market for calendars, you would not want to lump these groups together because you would be mixing too wide of a range of value relationships as you researched the subject. It would be much better to give each group its own category, perhaps in terms of their calendar usage.

We have found that the simplest market segmentations are those that use criteria where the segments are described using some assortment of industry descriptions. We like this because there is a large amount of information available on industries both on the Web and in industry-related media and trade shows. That is important because having the ability to tap into large amounts of secondary information electronically can greatly speed up your segmentation analysis and significantly add to your fact base.

SEGMENTATION IS AN ITERATIVE PROCESS

We are often asked when should a segmentation analysis be done. The best answer to that is always. Segmentation is an iterative process. You can do it initially in a broad sense, looking across a lot of different markets for segments that seem to have the most appeal. Next, you can do a deep dive into a single segment, where you first break it down into subsegments that you analyze in depth. You can do it well in advance of having your first product in the market, just before you launch your new product, and again a short time after launching. Since marketing is such a rapidly changing business, each time you do it you will see another dimension and you will learn more. The important thing to do is to develop an initial segmentation model and then to update it continuously as you learn more information about your markets.

THE 80/20 RULE OF MARKET SEGMENTS

It is a fact, for most innovative products and services, the bulk of the early business will be built from just a handful of markets. It is one of those 80/20 rules—80 percent of the success will come from 20 percent of the all the market segments. There are a lot of reasons why this rule generally holds up, but the strongest reason is economic. What is interesting to customers in one segment may not have equal value to customers in another. Today's innovation customers are mostly concerned with competing within their industry segment and are interested in new technologies that help accomplish this. In the past, there was the situation where many products had broad appeal across many segments because the needs to get connected were common across diverse segments. But as this phase passed, there has been more interest in spending for creating strategic advantage through investment in innovations that are unique to an industry sector. As such, the technologies that are of great interest to customers in a particular segment may be of lesser interest to others. Consequently, success with an innovative product, especially in the initial phases of market development, is most likely to have the greatest yield from a few segments.

We have found that this rule holds for most product categories with few exceptions. This can be really good news for marketers since, as we will show you shortly, it should be relatively straightforward to decide in the early phases of product development which segments are going to be the most lucrative.

A year before you introduce your new product you should be able to determine exactly which markets are going to account for 80 percent of your initial sales, and what the customers in these segments value most about what your product does. Imagine how you can use this advance knowledge to improve your ability to win market share for your innovation.

CHICKEN AND EGGS, HORSES AND CARTS

A common problem that innovators have is deciding who their audience is. In the early days of a new idea, it is often not clear what type of

customers will most want the product: Will the customers be big companies or small companies? Is it something that separate departments
will want or is it something for an entire organization? Will North
American customers want it more than those in other markets? Early on
you question which comes first. Does the product determine the market
or vice versa? One of the biggest benefits of doing market segmentation
early in the process, while your product ideas are still in their initial
development phases, is that segmentation develops a profile for the
largest set of initial customers, more or less providing a center of gravity
for what the development teams are building. And by doing so, it can
determine which customers will be most interested and why.

It is not uncommon for a group working on an innovative product
to flounder a bit because they are not exactly sure who the customers
are for a product. Early in your process you do not really know a lot
about who is going to use your new product and under what conditions. When there is little known about the customers, it is easy for a
development team to flail back and forth as they get pulled in con-
tradictory directions regarding product functionality. Segmentation
provides a simple way out of this dilemma. Since it is a process designed to expose the majority of customers for a new product, it
provides the ability to focus on a preliminary group of customers that
seems to "matter" more than others.

In a sense, segmentation provides an anchor by giving you a customer reference point. The segmentation process gives a voice to
customer demand in the early stages of development. While this may
not be a perfect representation of the potential customer base, it is
better than not having one at all. Of course, you can refine this ori-
entation over time.

DO MORE IN EACH MARKET SEGMENT

We are not advocates of building a business strategy based solely on
market segmentation. Just because we tell you that it is really important to get your segmentation strategy right, it does not mean that we
are saying you should treat your business solely in terms of the segmentation results. But we do think that it is important to take extra
steps to foster your success in the most important market segments.

If you are a bit cool on the idea of market segmentation, then take it
one step at a time. Imagine that you are going to try to figure out just

one change that you can make for your biggest market segment. Just one change—an additional feature, an additional salesperson covering a specific set of prospects, a business partner, an additional trade show to go to, or an additional publication to advertise in—and set the goal of that change as the objective for completing the first iteration of a market segmentation strategy. Since you have a modest goal, then do not put a lot of time into this first iteration—maybe take a half day at on an offsite meeting to give this a try. If you like the results, then go for the next iteration.

While it may not seem like a lot, making a change or two to capitalize on some advanced information that you may learn regarding key segments can yield a pretty big payback. For an NBA team, one player can make a huge difference. In professional football, coaches work hard at studying the competition and design plays to take advantage of mismatches. Similarly, market segmentation can ferret out important distinct advantages you can turn into opportunities. Football teams use special teams to perform during kickoffs and punt returns. You can apply a parallel process for dealing with unique segment situations. Through the anticipation process, you are able to identify demand shifts in key segments before they occur. This provides the opportunity to adjust your strategies ahead of changing market conditions. Since you developed the view of your segmentation strategies through the anticipation process—through direct interactions with experts in real-world situations—you are able to go back to these experts and ask them to help interpret market nuances which you may be able to turn into an advantage.

SEGMENTATION LETS YOU ADAPT TO MARKET CONDITIONS

One of the most important attributes of a market share leader is its ability to adapt to changing market conditions. Most changes start from within one or two segments. Changes in the market open up opportunities for getting and keeping new customers making it important to identify changes early. Even broad-based market changes will appear in one or two market segments before they spread across other industry sectors. So, staying on top of the important market segments is worth doing not just for the sake of a particular segment but also for the broad-based market as well.

SEGMENTATION AS A SALES STRATEGY

It is pretty common for sales teams to divide across geographic lines. Considering the logistics involved with developing customer relations on a face-to-face basis, it makes a lot of sense to match sales territories to major metropolitan cities. But in the early days of selling a new product line, dividing along market segments may be a better strategy. Since 80 percent of a new product's sales are likely to fall into a handful of market segments, having sales teams that are experts on these market segments can provide customers with the most "advanced" knowledge of the potential benefits of using your new product in their businesses. Doing this lets you sell "deep" into these market segments, since they will yield the most. Using sales specialists trained on the segments goes a long way toward helping to bridge the gap between what you do and market.

SEGMENTATION AS A DEFENSIVE STRATEGY

The funny thing about market segmentation is that if you do not put segmentation to work for your company, one of your competitors will do just that and begin to take market opportunities away from you until you respond. It is one of those business paradoxes—you are going to do it one way or the other. Either you figure out your segmentation strategy in advance and differentiate your products to match specific market conditions, or you will be chasing your competitors who figure it out before you do and put you in catch-up mode.

So even if you are one of those who do not think that segmentation is the holy grail of marketing of innovative products, then do it as part of your competition strategy because they will force you to do it anyway.

DOING MORE WITH LESS

Since segmentation is a process that lets you focus on the most important part of your business opportunity, it lets you shed those activities that do not have as much relevance. The famous quote in 1886 from legendary retailer John Wanamaker—"I know that 50% of my advertising is wasted. I just don't know which half" applies here. You know that there are a lot of things that you might be doing that are wasteful but you are unsure of which ones to eliminate.

Segmentation addresses these issues by developing clear market objectives early in the innovation cycle. If the segments are well understood during the product development process, resources can be efficiently applied to producing a success for customers in these markets.

THE ANTICIPATION PROCESS FOR MARKET SEGMENTATION

As you will see in a moment, our market segmentation methodology is a variation of our anticipation process. This methodology works to first bring together through a brainstorming process all of the segment possibilities, eliminating the weakest candidates and then using Expert Interviews to help discern the best segment opportunities. We have developed a scoring process to rank the strengths of each of the individual segments and provide a comparison across a set of analyzed segments.

Step 1: Selecting the Alternatives

Group brainstorm. Organize your group and develop a master list of all the possible applications for your product along with the segments that will use these products. Brainstorming processes vary depending on the team dynamics, but the overall purpose of the process is to delineate all of the possible market segments and then logically group them into clusters based on some set of common criteria.

Eliminate the weakest segments. It may sound strange after having just brainstormed the possibilities, but the very first thing you should do with the master list of segments that you have created is to eliminate the ones that you already know to be weak markets. Your time is valuable and the fewer markets that you will analyze in depth, the better.

Determine the size of each segment. For the segments that remain, find something to count. We like to quantify the size of each of the remaining markets segments. Obviously, the thing that you count should have some relationship to the economic potential of the market segment from the perspective of your product, so what you count is important. But it is important to include, at this point, some hard facts relating to the size of the market—number of customers, number of Fortune 500 companies in the segment, how big are their revenues, what do they spend on technology or your type of product, how many locations to they have. Whatever you choose, identify the sizing element for each segment (what you count does not have to be the same for each segment but it will help if it's similar).

Begin building the fact base through online searches. Electronically research the application ideas within the segment to find articles about these applications. Develop a list of the key publications and trade shows within each segment. For the segments that look like they have lots of potential, you may even want to attend the trade shows to expand your fact base.

Competitive analysis. Research others supplying similar or complimentary products to the market segments. Competitors often post their reference accounts on their Web sites along with stories about how their clients are using their products.

Create a database of experts. As you are doing the above steps, compile a database of names that crop up from industry articles, user groups, industry analysts, trade publication editors and writers, Web portal proprietors, reference accounts, and competitors' experts.

Step 2: Expert Interviews

Discussion guide. Before you begin interviews, it is helpful to develop a discussion guide that you will use to complete the interviews. This should not be a precise set of questions as you might do with a survey questionnaire. Your questions should be more open-ended because you are looking to understand the nature of the market segment that your expert operates in for the purpose of determining the potential that this segment may hold for your product.

Segment scoring matrix. In this step, we ask you to score the market segments to rank order the results of your findings. To help do this, during this step, you will want to include in your Expert Interview discussion topics that will help you with your scoring. As we have mentioned previously, we use six topics to help assess market strengths. Incorporating some of these questions in your discussion guide may improve your discussions:

1. *Need:* What is the application? What problem does your product solve for people in the industry?
2. *Value:* What is the value? How valuable is it to solve this problem (and is there any simple way to measure this value or describe it to others)?
3. *Volume:* What is the size? How many people in this segment have this problem, and what might they be willing to pay for the solution?
4. *Complete product:* What is required to satisfy the need? Does your product completely solve the problem, or are there other steps that the customer must take or other products and services that the customer must buy in order to solve the problem?
5. *Channel:* What is the sales channel that your expert would expect to be used to fulfill the need?
6. *Marketing communications:* How do people in the segment hear about new products and services? Which industry conferences do they go to? Are there user groups that are important? What do they read? Which companies occupy the leading positions in the market and why?

Expert Interviews. Using names developed during the preceding step and the expanded discussion guide discussed above, interview experts in the segments.

Step 3: Scoring

Scoring. Using our six scoring elements—need, value, volume, complete product offering, channel, and positioning/marketing communications—score each of the segments that you have studied. So, if you are looking at five market segments, then you are building a matrix with thirty cells in it. Since you are dealing with a lot of qualitative information, the scoring part becomes a little weird because you have to convert the qualitative information into a score. So keeping it simple will make it easier for you. The way we do it is to use a scale of 1 to 10, where 1 means that what you heard was not really very positive for the market and 10 means that the answers you got implied a terrific fit. When you are finished scoring, you can add up the scores for each of the segments to form an overall ranking. If you want to get fancy about this, you can also apply a weighting question to each of the criteria (we generally weigh the first three categories—need, value, and volume—higher than the last three). By now you probably get the idea—you have developed a strength matrix to quantify the differences in the potential segments across a number of dimensions.

Top 100 customers. For the best segments, develop a profile of the best company characteristics—what characteristics makes one company a better potential than another? Using this sort of profiling technique, for each of the top segments you can identify the top prospects for your products within that segment. By doing this for a handful of segments, you can create a list of the top 100 customers for your new product. This list is important because not only does it help determine what your sales and channel strategy should be (now that you know who your top customers should be, it might be helpful to hire salespeople and channel partners that have definite experience selling to these companies), but it also gives you the ability to go back to experts in these companies with a second round of interviews with a simple question: "Here's what we're planning to build and we think that your company probably will want to buy a lot of it, does this make sense to you?"

Displaying. As they say, "a picture is worth a thousand words." It is helpful to be able to display the results of your segmentation work in a chart form to communicate to others in your organization which markets are important to you and why. We have found two formats helpful for doing this. The first chart is a simple bar chart showing the results of your segment scorings, starting with the leading segment. The second chart is a quadrant chart showing two dimensions—the strength of the segment compared with the ability for your company to sustain differentiation in the other dimension. The upper-right quadrant should contain the most interesting segments—those that hold lots of economic potential for you and where your company will have a long-term competitive differentiation.

DISCARD THE ZAMBONIES

In the first segmentation step we ask you to pick the "universe" of possible segments and then quickly discard the ones that are too small to care about. It is important to use your time wisely, so eliminating segments that do not offer much in the way of an opportunity lets you spend more time on the important ones.

You want to look for alternatives that are interesting, but under even casual scrutiny have little real economic potential. They are the Zambonies. A Zamboni is that cool truck that resurfaces ice between hockey periods. Now, Zambonies are really interesting and are elegant examples of a purpose-engineered machine, but the demand for ice rink surface machines will not spike unless a new ice age descends.

So, in spite of its widespread brand recognition and dominating market share, Zamboni ice resurfacers are not a good business platform because they represent a relatively small market with little growth likely. Making floor mats or custom steering wheels for a Zamboni will probably not send your kids to college. Just because it has an interesting application does not mean that it packs the punch that goes along with surging markets.

After looking for the Zambonies and discarding segments that may be interesting but will not enable you to score big, look for segments that represent opportunities that are likely to take lots of work but will not produce much return. Discarding low-yielding segments at this stage helps improve the effectiveness of what you will be doing in the subsequent stages. By eliminating the weakest ideas, you will get to spend more of your energy on the stronger ones. Since the steps that follow involve a more detailed and time-consuming examination of each of the remaining segments, reducing their number at this point means you will have more time to spend on understanding and anticipating the future of the remaining segments.

KEEPING IT SIMPLE

When done right, segmentation should be simple. The entire segmentation process is designed to take something that is very complicated (marketing to the entire universe) and simplify it to the point where you end up describing a credible opportunity on which a firm with your resources can execute (marketing to a few specific targets).

You should try to get market segmentation to the point where an eleven year old can understand it.

Because of the nature of their products, semiconductor companies usually have the simplest segmentation strategies. Most semi-conductors are designed for very targeted applications, and they are sold to manufacturers. For instance, if your company is designing a new chip that combines a cellular radio and a global positioning receiver, then your customers are surely going to be companies that manufacture cell phones, and the market size is going to be a subset of the global market for cell phones. Good market segmentation for a semiconductor company usually sounds something like this: We will soon be producing this chip that *this list of manufacturers* may use in their next-generation product that they sell to *those types of customers*. While the *this list* and *those types* change from chip to chip, the clarity that comes through from a semiconductor market segmentation is brilliant. It is our hope that you reach this same level with your own segmentation.

Concluding a segmentation analysis with a very simple statement is a wonderful way of describing your overall business strategy in plain and simple terms so that others inside and outside of your organiza-tion understand. One simple way to wrap up a segmentation analysis is to describe the three most important market segments that you think are important, and then, within these segments, pick one or two things that are most important for your company to achieve. So you end up saying something like: "For our newest product, we have found that we add significant value in markets A, B, and C while simultaneously offering something that these customers can't get elsewhere and, to gain traction in these markets, we must take the following two steps." This is both simple and powerfully effective.

DON'T ASK US WHY SOME PEOPLE
DON'T LIKE SEGMENTATION

We cannot tell you how many times we have run into the problem that many people involved with innovative products and services do not like market segmentation. In fact, you might say that they actually hate it. We meet these people all the time. Gener-ally, there are three types of people that do not like to segment their markets:

1. Drowners—Marketers who think that it is best to jump in the water and learn to swim. Our sympathies to their companies because they are just wasting precious time.

2. Engineer turned Marketer—Alas, many bright people who should know better think that marketing is something that almost anyone with a laptop can do. Since so many innovative companies are run by engineers, you see this happen a lot, even at the highest levels of management. One of the best ways that separates great engineers from average ones is their empirical reasoning—they learn by trial and error. Consequently, they think it is only natural to apply this same reasoning to marketing, leaving them generally unable to do any real marketing until their product is about ready for beta testing. They are too comfortable in this mode, so they automatically assume that they are doing everything just right if they apply the same principles that made them great engineers to the marketing aspects of their business. Big mistake.

3. Venture investors—Ill-informed investors often feel that diving too deeply into the area of market segmentation will somehow devalue their investment by limiting the size of the market opportunity. Investors generally want to have broad-based successes because they will produce the highest valuations. In general, there is nothing wrong with this reasoning—the more broad-based the market opportunity the greater the return. What they fail to see is that market segmentation is perfectly consistent with producing a broad-based business opportunity if it is used to provide a foundation for later growth.

THE ROLE OF THE KILLER APP

When we are hearing about an innovative new product we'll often ask, "so now that we understand what you are doing, can you kindly tell us about some of the killer apps that really wow customers?" We often get a really negative reaction to that question. It seems the idea of "killer apps" is kind of a dirty word, and if you cannot figure it out for yourself, then you needed to ask the question—one that seems obvious to the company (or embarrassing to them if they have not quite figured it out yet for themselves). We think that the question of whether something you are working on is a killer app is a really good way to make the leap from a discussion about an interesting technology to the much bigger subject of how does this technology actually impacts its users. Yet finding your killer apps is a very difficult problem.

Killer apps are few and far between. That is why financial markets generously reward innovative companies that discover them. Conversely, if killer apps were a dime a dozen, then finding them would not be so hard and the rewards would not be so high.

Taking a deep dive look into the most important market segments is the best way that we have found for discovering your killer apps. There are a couple of reasons why this is true. First of all, as we have already said, certain markets, for reasons that are unique to those markets, will be more interested in what you do than other markets. Those markets are the ones that have the most to gain by using what you are making. Second, since you are likely to face asymmetrical markets, you will need to yield more from a few select markets in order to make your financial plan.

Given that some markets care more and consequently may pay more for what you are proposing to do, why not go out of your way to try to better understand how participants in these markets will interact with your innovation? Suppose, for instance, that you have determined that companies in the financial services markets will be one of the key market segments for the widget you have invented. Then why not take a deeper look at the financial services market and imagine, for a few minutes, that this is the *only* market that you are in which you are going to be operating. Using our anticipation process, what if you applied a lot of in depth expert interviews into finding out just how embedded your widget might become in that industry and what some of the ways that people in those markets would use your product? What if the whole world revolved around your idea, and what if customers could deploy your innovation at every conceivable place? And what if you could spend what it took to make your innovation have a significant impact for your customers? What changes might result? How would your customer's business improve? What will be different about your customer's business? How would you go about restructuring what you are doing to help better make these changes to your customers' business come about?

By defining your killer app in terms of a single market instead of across a whole range of markets, you gain the advantage of narrowing your perspective to a single market. By doing so you greatly improve your chances of understanding your innovation's potential impact, since you are able to view your impact from a very specific perspective. Of course, our Expert Interview methodology lets you make this analysis more than just a thought exercise. So in a way, the entire anticipation process—including segmentation strategy—is designed to help find your killer app. If you can find a killer app, everything usually falls right into place.

Chapter 9

Finding the Next Big Thing

You miss 100% of the shots you don't take.

—Wayne Gretzky

Spinsters

Lots of companies tell us a story that goes something like this: "We just met with the chief information officer (CIO) of a big Fortune 500 company. He told us that this is the first time that he's seen a company doing what we're doing and that he really likes the idea. We know we're onto something really big." We do not mind companies like this that hype their ideas by spinning tales about how they have remarkable solutions never before seen. But it really surprises us when people actually start *believing* their own hype. The trouble with these sorts of statements is that if the CIO of the big Fortune 500 company had never seen this sort of thing, then that input really may not be very relevant. Assuming that the CIO is a reasonably competent executive, the reason he never had seen this sort of thing was, maybe, because he was not looking for it, perhaps because it was not really important to his company's business mission. Like most human beings, entrepreneurial executives often hear what they want to hear. It is quite likely that the CIO was merely being polite and not nearly as enthusiastic as they would like to think. So when we listen to these sorts of mindless statements what we actually hear is—"We just talked to someone who doesn't really give a darn about this topic and he thought it was a cool idea but totally irrelevant to his business problems."

On Demand

Starting in 2002, IBM launched an initiative they named their On Demand Computing initiative, backing it with a whopping $10 billion investment. During the boom of the 1990s, IBM effectively used an overarching strategy dubbed "e-Business" to position the company, its products, and its services as a credible business partner for helping organizations adapt to the changes wrought by the growth of the Internet. On Demand Computing has become the new marketing vehicle that IBM is using to position itself in the minds of its customers.

IBM is not the only computer company pushing a high-level vision of flexible computing, but it certainly seems to be the most effective player. Looking across the computing industry, almost all of the major hardware and software vendors are promoting "utility computing" in one form or another. HP is positioning itself around what it calls UDC—Utility Data Center. Sun has its N1 strategy designed to let customers get more out of its computers by auto-mating tasks. Software giant Veritas calls their version Utility Now. You can go through the positioning of most of the big hardware and software vendors and find their attempts to weave the concepts of utility computing into their positioning messages.

But while IBM's competitors are focusing on the utility aspects of their product lines through clever switch of words, IBM transforms the concept from "what it is" to "what impact it can have." This conforms to the traditional marketing maxim of talking about benefits rather than features. This is a foundation principle of sound marketing strategy that is ignored too often, especially by innova-tors in love with their own technology. The words "On Demand" actually form a two-headed positioning strategy. Used to describe its products, On Demand has all of the aspects of utility computing and more as substantiated by IBM's autonomic computing initia-tives. Used to describe the effect that it has on a business, On Demand is used to define the attributes of a modern business—one whose business processes are so well integrated across the com-pany and with key partners, suppliers, and customers that the business can respond with flexibility and speed to any customer demand, market opportunity, or threat. So while their competitors may be promising hardware and software that works continuously like a utility plant is supposed to do, IBM is providing customers with the ability to transform their businesses to be flexible enough to meet whatever customer demands or market threats that suddenly loom.

Not only did IBM pick a very clever positioning vehicle, they also seemed to do everything right when it brought this positioning message out into the market. They took the time to get their employees up to speed on what On Demand meant. Positioning will not work if you cannot get your own workforce to buy in to the concept, and IBM continues to work hard to "sell" the concepts throughout its own workforce. Each division of the company gave meaning to On Demand in its own way. By backing the On Demand initiatives with a huge research budget, and by using the concepts of autonomic computing as the technical foundation, IBM was able to drive innovation across not only its products but those of its partners. And, of course, by effectively and continuously communicating its concepts of On Demand computing, IBM effectively gave meaning to On Demand from the customer's very own perspective.

You cannot deny it. That is pretty powerful stuff making it really hard for competitors to counter.

DISRUPTION

We get press releases and product announcements of great ambitions all the time about some new start-up that has just received a gazillion dollars of new funding, including a quote from their CEO saying: "We have a disruptive technology that addresses the pent-up demand of enterprises for...[insert whatever it is that they are making here]...thus giving us a broad platform upon which to build a presence across numerous enterprise markets and set the agenda for the industry." Boy, we cannot tell you how these sorts of statements spin the needle of our "snake oil meter." We really wish that we had tracked the number of times that senior executives at innovative companies tell us that they are working on a "disruptive technology" that is going to "change the rules" in their industry—and so on and so forth. The only redemptive value in hearing this is that we are pretty certain that it only takes about a year for companies making these broad claims to whither away, making us eager to enjoy the industrial entertainment factor they present while we can. After all, many of these companies have been funded with millions of dollars in venture money (often coming from your mother's pension fund), so if the food they are serving at their press launch is pretty good, we might as well enjoy it before it gets cold.

Maybe you are asking the same question that we do: Is there a reason why these companies cannot just come out and tell people what they are doing in a clear and simple manner? All of the rhetoric about having a disruptive technology and becoming the platform for the future more or less gets in the way of telling their story.

The executives who run these companies and those that finance them are bright people. But their egos get in the way. Everyone wants to find the NBT (next big thing). That is where the money is. At one level you can say that is why you are involved with these sorts of exciting technologies in the first place. They are revolutionary. They offer a chance of changing important aspects of society. There is no denying that the Internet has changed communications as we know it. Face it, this world is an exciting one. And if you are like us and are totally absent the talents that could make you famous or wealthy by being in movies or becoming the next Tiger Woods, then you are looking at this technology stuff and saying, "This is my ticket to ride!"

In his book, *The Innovator's Dilemma*, Clayton Christensen used the words "disruptive technology" to contrast against a sustaining technology—a radical versus incremental distinction. Those of us lucky enough to be part of a disruptive event have the ability to become participants as a major new market develops.

Finding a disruptive technology is really important stuff, because that is where the big bucks (and often the fame and recognition) are. Companies at the scene of the crime of a disruptive technology stand the best chance of getting a big ROI because they are able to capitalize on changing market conditions. Disruptions are the things that knock the big companies out of the game and open the way for innovative companies to take over large parts of the market. So finding the disruption and being there at the right time can yield a Google-sized return. Who would not want to be there? And of course, executives at the scene also will get a huge boost on the ego meters as they take yet another start-up down that road of success.

Many of these executives might want to actually *read* Clayton Christensen's book before they start self-declaring their companies to be the discoverers of a disruption in the market. It turns out that it takes more than issuing a press release declaring that your innovation is a disruptive event. In the early phases, disruptive technologies go through a difficult period as their markets are quite pale in comparison to well-established sustaining technologies. Disruptive technologies typically are simpler, cheaper, first commercialized in emerging or insignificant markets, and generally not interesting to the most profitable customer segments of the sustaining technology. And the customers for disruptive technologies are not the customers from the mainstream markets. In fact, mainstream customers most likely will reject the disruptive innovations as not being "good enough." Innovators need to find new markets in order for their products to get traction.

NEXT BIG THING

Finding the NBT is not easy. The really good ones are few and far between. Of course, the example that we all have in our heads for the NBT is the Internet, and that presents another problem: We are unlikely to experience another NBT the size of the Internet in our lifetimes. Maybe our children's children will have that pleasure—perhaps when time travel or molecular transport a la *Star Trek* is introduced. And of course, the Internet took twenty-five years or so to develop from an interesting lab project to become the basis for reengineering communications as we knew it. Given that reality, it turns out that any of us would be happy if we could find a more modest NBT just in the marketplace in which we are working.

All kidding aside, many of us can chronicle our careers in terms of the proximity to an assortment of NBT events that we encountered over the years. As participants in the innovation business, we have all been influenced by the NBTs that we have encountered, both those that have actually succeeded and those that have fizzled, because they create so much energy in the market from both customers and investors.

Of course, our advice to you on your quest to find your very own NBT is to use our anticipation process to help you on your journey. The whole idea of the anticipation process is to get a look at what is ahead and then drive that learning into your business plans. It naturally follows that the anticipation process should help you in seeing whether something that you are working on really is the NBT.

If the idea that you are considering is part of the NBT, then consider the impact that the next big thing will have on the market. NBTs really are disruptive. Ultimately, NBTs can really only be measured by the impact they have on markets. A market that really is or was huge will be totally thrown for a loop by the NBT. Consider the influence of DVDs on the way movies are marketed or the i-Pod's influence on music sales. When you are looking to develop your concept of whether something is or is not the NBT, you are looking for something that we refer to as the truck coming down the road. Think of the NBT in terms of a truck off in the distance, and you are trying to determine how big the truck is, how far away it is, how fast it is going, and if it is headed in your direction. If you dream of this thing being your NBT, then the truck you are looking for had better give you some indication that it is out there in the distance and coming your way. If you cannot get any information that confirms the truck is moving your way, then maybe what you're working on, while it may be important and it may be financially viable, is not quite the NBT you had hoped.

Since NBTs disrupt big markets, then a couple of very good questions that you can ask yourself are: "If this really is the NBT, then exactly which markets are going to get disrupted and which companies are the most exposed (who may be the biggest losers)?" Using the Internet as a reference point for this NBT discussion, you could see early in the process that the big losers were going to be the telco companies (such as AT&T and the local providers) whose entire infrastructures predated the Internet and needed to be reengineered in the event that the Internet actually took off. The most important attribute of an NBT event is that it is supposed to be, in fact, *big,* and big is something that you can look for.

Getting back to our truck metaphor, if what you are looking for is really going to be big, then at what point does it first appear on the horizon? Even when it is off in the distance, you should be able to see something coming, albeit faintly. If you have a sense for what will be disrupted (which companies will be impacted), then at least you know what direction the disruption is possibly headed in. The Linux operating system is another good example of a disruption that had a direction. Whether or not you believed Linux was going to be commercially popular, there were several targets that stood to be the "disruptees"— Sun, HP, IBM, and Microsoft. As Linux gained momentum, HP and IBM deftly moved aside (by actually jumping on the Linux bandwagon, realizing that they could actually gain from the disruption), while Sun unfortunately stayed right in the middle of the road waiting as the Linux truck started to mow them down. As of this writing, Microsoft is a bit further down the road, still figuring out how to handle the potential impact of Linux on its markets.

As analysts, we have figured out that an important part of our jobs is to entertain our clients—give them a break from their nine-to-five boredom. (We found this out when we hired an intern who had put himself through college being a stand-up comic—although he had little in the way of technology experience, his sense of audience timing during client presentations had our clients asking for him.) Participating in an analyst briefing is a lot better than going to the next human resource meeting. As analysts, we have learned it makes for great storytelling to talk about disruptions that hit markets with little warning. While many want to believe that technology disruptions come "out of nowhere" to shake up important markets, we know this not to be the case. Why? The disruption itself has to incubate in some sort of customer preemergent laboratory. Sometime, well in advance of the disruption taking hold, the disruptive technology has to add value to some small set of customer situations. While in the fashion industry it might be possible for a designer to launch a new trend with a runway show at the Paris spring show, it is just not the case that innovation driven disruptions hit the market on a moment's notice—at some level the trends may have been apparent for at least awhile. They have to begin somewhere. And they have got to grow in some market. We have shown you our methods to identify and track experts who may be at the "scenes" of these disruptions. It is up to you to determine just what it is you are finding—is it a truck in the distance, is it coming your way, will it have major impact on traffic patterns, and how can you use it to your advantage?

Lots of times you will look at things, and after debating whether or not it is a possible disruption, you will decide that it probably is not. Keep in mind that "probably not" is most often the correct answer. Disruptions are not everyday events. Real market disruptions create lots of opportunity for nimble innovative companies to make a fortune. If disruptions were more frequent, there would be many more successes than you see in today's economy. There would be many more successful venture investors. There would be many more "Silicon Valley" scenarios around the world. The reality is that they are few and far between.

Having realized that you are working on the NBT, then start your anticipation process by profiling the characteristics that a successful NBT will have over the next few years. If it really is going to be the NBT, then you can probably anticipate now who the major business partners will be for your innovation. Since it is the NBT, you will have the cream-of-the-crop of business partners available to help with distribution, market development, and strategic development. And of course, over time, you will acquire the most important customers in these areas, so add this list to your anticipation working group. The next step, of course, is to use interviews with the experts among this working group to determine just how your NBT may evolve as it moves out of the innovation lab and into the mainstream market. Using our truck metaphor, at this point you are trying to figure out the route that the truck (currently off in the horizon) will take.

We encourage you to be really skeptical whenever you are considering whether something is or is not an NBT. Our basic philosophy is that if something big is going to happen, it does not come out of nowhere. In aviation the term "under the radar" has real meaning—a plane is flying below the level at which radar sensors can detect it. That does not mean that the plane does not exist. Nor does it mean that the plane cannot be tracked. It simply means that the plane cannot be detected using conventional means. We are encouraging you to draw a parallel between this example and your quest to identify the NBT. If something is going to be big in the not too distant future, then there must be evidence available to support this belief. And conventional methods may not be able to detect it. Nevertheless, this should not stop you from using unconventional methods like our anticipation process to develop a set of observations that you can use to anticipate the future.

Once you have your NBT, figuring out how to tell the world about it is another matter. Over the past decade, the technology industry has developed into a sort of mini-version of the motion picture industry. There are many parallels between the way that Hollywood goes about the business of financing and promoting a new hit movie and the way that technology companies launch their innovations. Perhaps it is because of the similarities between financing a major movie and financing a technology start-up: Both industries use high-risk venture investing to fund projects that generally last from two to five years. What is different is that marketing Hollywood blockbusters is a much better developed discipline than is the marketing of innovative new products. Blockbuster marketing has almost become a science in terms of getting a return on the production investment from theaters, DVDs, promotional tie-ins, thrill rides, video game licensing, and more. Using only a few indicators, Hollywood marketers can accurately gauge the potential of a new release and, using these indicators, act accordingly. If the movie looks like it is going to be a blockbuster, they will do a huge buildup prior to the release. If it is a going to be a dog, they will limit their losses, keep critics away until it is released (suckering people in to the opening weekend), and go quickly to DVD sales. In the world of innovation, there is less discipline in the process; each new product seems to take on a life of its own as if there were no precedent in the area.

We are, of course, advocating that this should not be the case. That is why we believe our profiling process for identifying in advance ultimate success factors (characteristics of success—company structure, customers, markets, sales channel, strategic partners . . .) for an innovative new product is so important. The advantage of profiling is the ability to go directly to the ultimate sources needed to support an innovation's market success to determine its viability well in advance of the release of the product. If it is going to be a huge success, there should be plenty of evidence if you look in the right places. It might be that the traditional customers are not going to form the early market for an innovation and that the places where you are going to get validation for the concept will come from new customers putting the product to new uses. Nevertheless, by developing the profiles for the ultimate impact that a NBT can have and by completing expert discussions with those identified through the profiling process, you will be able to determine whether you are working on something that has blockbuster potential or might otherwise be just a blip on the industry's radar.

Our Dos and Don'ts List for Analyst Briefings

Analyst firms play an interesting role in the modern world of information technology. In the good old days the major system vendors like IBM would take care of their major customers in the case of a bad decision that IBM had promoted. There was real substance to the phrase: "You never get fired for buying from IBM." The modern world of open systems and vendor interchangeability has changed all of that. System vendor profit margins have been whittled down to the point that they cannot provide this kind of cradle-to-grave support to their loyal customers. Analyst firms have jumped in to partially fill this void by providing independent viewpoints that assist decision—making regarding technology deployments and to assist the trade press as they develop articles and news stories about your industry. People do not buy technology based on ads they read. That may be how they find about them. But when they are considering purchases, they check with friends and look for recommendations from people they trust. This is where industry analysts come in. They play an important role this process by explaining to customers and the media the ownership issues associated with new innovations.

So as part of telling the world about your next big thing, you have to brief analysts and they end up listening to countless briefings. From that receiver perspective here is our list of do's and don'ts for briefing analysts like us.

Dos

1. Know what you want to say. Remember, we get lots of these briefings and necessarily forget most of the details or never hear them in the first place. Be as clear as possible in your own mind what few key points you want to make and have stick.

2. Make those points quickly. You have at most ten minutes while people are listening before they start doing their e-mail or sending sarcastic IM messages to one another about how bored they are. Omit the philosophy and background. None of those first ten minutes should be wasted.

3. Answer the basic questions. How big is the market (tell us why we should care), how are you different, and how does your business model let you win? If all you do is answer these three questions, then your presentation will be a success.

4. Teach. Help us understand the space better and in an interesting way. Analysts are always looking for new ideas to include in the next report. Explain the problem in an interesting and innovative way, and if you are lucky, the analyst will steal what you tell them and use it in their work. If they promote a problem for which you have the solution you have gone a long way to making the visit worthwhile.

5. Know where we come from before you arrive. Management teams regularly come to our office without the foggiest idea what we care about. It only takes a minute or two to do a Google search to get a good idea of who you are about to talk to. Hey, if we are going to spend an hour of our time listening, then give us a break and at least find out what we have been doing.

6. Tell us how you fit in. There are many of big players in the technology world that exert a lot of influence on customers. We

want to know how your company will succeed despite (or because of) the presence of the big players.

Don'ts

1. Don't bring a big entourage. Do not bring along someone if all he or she is going to do is sit there and smile. Focus the meeting on your target audience and get the most out of their time.

2. Don't quote other analysts. It is rude and not at all productive. Just as you compete with others, so, too, do the analyst firms, and they really do not like one another (go ahead, call all of us petty if you want).

3. No brown nosing. Do not ask for our opinion unless you really want it and are willing to hear our input. If you do not care about someone's opinion, why are you talking to them in the first place? If you do care and ask, listen to what they say and acknowledge that you heard it (you do not have to agree with it). From time to time we seem to really offend companies by giving critical feedback to a weak presentation. If you do not want the feedback, then do not ask. We are sure it is not the most pleasant experience, but it is a lot more pleasant than having your product bomb in the marketplace.

4. Don't do all the talking. We have this saying that the person who talks the most during a meeting always feels that the meeting was a good one, and we have had plenty of briefings where people must go away feeling good because they had did not let anyone else get a word in. It does not really bother us when someone talks nonstop through a briefing; we have plenty of e-mail to catch up on.

5. Don't tell us something that we have heard before. Junior salespeople are told that if they go into a customer's office and see a mounted swordfish on the wall to never ask their customer about it; they are guaranteed to get a really long answer that their customer has probably told a thousand times before. In other words, it wastes everyone's time. We have groups come in all the time and have a half-dozen slides telling us things that we have heard a million times before like "the Internet is growing" or that "security is a problem." Don't waste time pointing out the crudely obvious.

6. Don't slam the competition. We get pretty tired of people coming by and telling us that their competitors are a bunch of dopes. The funny thing is that many of the guys coming by badmouthing their competitors eventually end up jumping ship and going to work for the very companies they were disparaging. We know most of the companies in your business are made up of people just like you. So keep your opinions of the competition to yourself.

WHAT'S AROUND THE CORNER?

We are always curious about what the next big innovation areas are going to be in the information technology world. The venture-funded companies that come to talk to us have often been funded primarily on the basis of claimed technological innovation. It helps us greatly if we independently develop a view of the most important information technology innovation vectors that the leading information technology customers are moving on so we are better able to judge the potency of new ideas.

It is striking to realize how dependent we have all become on computing infrastructure. Many years ago John Reed, then president of Citibank, said he was not sure whether Citibank was a financial institution that was using a network to provide a service, or whether Citibank was a networking company in the financial services vertical market; his bank and his network were inseparable. Ten years ago there were only a few companies whose businesses were so technologically intertwined and dependent. Today, it has become the norm. Modern companies—large, medium, and small—rely on their technology infrastructure to do business. Without it, they cease to function.

Much of this has come about because of the Internet, the standard networking protocols that enabled the interconnection of many different enterprises and other networks into one grand network system that spans the entire modern world. The Internet makes it possible to connect two computer systems anywhere in the world. The Web—standards for publishing and displaying information—means that a PC with a modern browser is all a user needs to access a remote application or information service. In a real sense all that the Internet and the Web offer is universal connectivity, but the impact is profound. Every successful business excels in part because of their execution of key business processes (e.g., supply chain management, customer relationship management, etc.). Because of the Internet, everyone who participates in that business process (employee, contractor, business partner, and customer alike) can collaborate using a shared network-accessed application. The result is a more efficient and more effective process, a competitive factor no company can afford to ignore. The Internet and the business process improvements network-accessed applications yield are the "high-order" bits in our model of the future. We need to refine it to the next level of detail in order to make the best use of it as an innovation foil.

First of all, let us offer a few cynical comments on what the future is not. No new technology should grab your attention if it is technology for technology's sake. (Remember the Segway? It was a great innovation and received a ton of publicity, but the market for it turned to be virtually nonexistent.) Smart people do not value their common sense enough. They think because they cannot understand the technical details of something new they must necessarily have to take the word of the technologist that it important and valuable. Hogwash! Do not trust anything where you cannot connect the dots and find the business value. Ask "Who cares and why?" early and often, and do not accept an answer that does not make business sense. The whole optical data bubble lacked fundamental common sense. An amazing amount of money was invested in Peer-to-Peer technologies without a clear understanding of what business problems it solved. New technology is a fool's paradise, especially if you do not trust your common sense when good answers are not forthcoming.

Technology cynicism notwithstanding, you can make sense out of much of the future, and, as you might assume, you should do it from the customer and business value perspective. Through that lens, the future of technical innovation looks remarkably bright and promising for a long time to come. As computers become more intertwined in an ongoing business, the applications really do become business critical—if the application is down, the employees are down, and the entire business is down. The impact on the operational aspects of IT is itself profound. With worldwide businesses and worldwide customers, the sun never sets on the business enterprise; there are no longer evenings or weekends for system maintenance. Applications need to be up 24/7 if the business is to be up 24/7. Traditional IT operational models are no longer adequate; IT needs to become significantly better and significantly cheaper. There is no shortage of innovation opportunities available.

Information security is another critical element for taking advantage of the opportunities presented by Internet connectivity. We find much of the discussion of security sadly off point. Information security is neither fundamentally an issue of dealing with external forces of evil nor one of dealing with governmentally enforced regulation compliance. If you want to really understand information security, you have to view it as the natural reflection of the increased value of the assets made available on the network. The more assets you put on the network, the more attention you have to spend assuring the integrity and privacy of those assets. It is a risk management problem, not a technology or governmental problem.

The final and in many ways overarching IT problem is operational cost and complexity. In the early days of computing, the cost of the technology limited use—you could not afford what you really wanted; you made do with what you could afford. The astounding and unprecedented technical progress in all aspects of computer technology has completely changed this. You can now afford all the computing equipment you could ever possibly need, but now you cannot afford to operate and administer it. During the dot com bubble, IT expenditures grew to a very visible part of the overhead costs in running an enterprise. There is now broad agreement that spending an ever-increasing percentage on IT is not a reasonable approach. IT expenditures need to be held in check or reduced. The big part of the cost is not the hardware, it is the people overhead. Reducing the administration and operational costs are key to progress—that is the only way of affording more technology and fundamentally better solutions. That is what is beneath the consolidation initiatives that have been broadly in place for the last few years.

The big picture we see is the seemingly paradoxical set of requirements: How do you simultaneously make information technology better (and more available), provide more security and with less complexity (and therefore make it less costly)? The first thing you do is take the management of IT much more seriously than it has been in the past. For the first fifty years the dominating challenge was just keeping up with technology's advantages and the application initiatives they presented. Today, more, faster, and cheaper is not good enough *by itself*. You have to be smarter too. What is beginning to happen in IT today, often under the banner of IT Service Management (ITSM), is analogous to what happened in American manufacturing twenty-five years ago when it was at risk of being clobbered by smart foreign companies that took process control and quality management more seriously than it did. Now, the same kind of management and process scrutiny is being placed on enterprise IT with the same astounding results. The simple goal is typically improved application (and business) availability, and the simple path to that goal is paying greater attention to how things are changed in order to minimize self-inflicted damage. The results begin with better availability and, as you might expect, lower costs as well. Along the way, an orderly attention to IT management also yields a way of seeing how all these issues and objectives are part of one big process and must be considered together if solutions are to be found. The first big vector we see driving customer needs is this need to make IT management and operations more orderly. It begins with a need to improve application availability, but along the way yields important benefits in operating costs and helps drive the administrative components of cost down so that more technology can be employed productively.

Security is the next big customer need vector that will drive innovation. Think of security as the sensible minimization of risk as we add more assets to the network. Remember that the goal is to enable productive use of those assets, not just make them safe. It is easy to design highly secure systems—the computer analogs of going to a bank and using a safety deposit box. There is little chance of information loss or compromise, and little chance of getting useful work done. Security is not a technical problem; distrust anyone who presents it that way. Making information secure starts with the challenging but absolutely necessary task of sorting out how an enterprise should use information. To make security work, information and services have to be easily usable for those who need it to get their jobs done, but not available to those who do not need it (the concept of "minimal privilege"). This is a simple idea that is amazingly hard to implement because along the way you have to really understand what work is and what it takes to get it done. And then you need system directories that can be queried for up-to-the-moment information and who can do what, and reflect the promotion or termination that happened very recently.

The final customer need vector is simplicity. What might sound like platitudinous consultant's advice is actually the key to understanding how this all works out. What we keep discovering is the problem of complexity. If you create a computer solution in 1995 and then look at it ten years later, it looks very different simply because all the technology improved thirty to fifty times during that period. Suppose the original system had 25 percent of the cost in technology. If we maintain that same cost ratio, then ten years later we have a lot more stuff and, since having more stuff is more complicated, and we now have to spend a lot more to manage and administer the greater amount of stuff. Given the continuing progress in technology, and assuming that we really want to take advantage of cheaper and faster computer systems—we want to use them—then unless we really focus on minimizing complexity, in the end it will limit what we can do. Simplicity is the clear key to minimizing the operational and administrative costs of IT. Simplicity is the most important means of making systems reliable and available. Simplicity makes effective security a lot easier; if all the system differences are meaningful, it is easier to see when something suspicious or anomalous is happening. Simplicity is the magic word.

These three customer-driven vectors—availability, security, and simplicity—are the hidden hands that will guide IT innovations for years to come. Intel will continue to build faster processors because otherwise their profitable business collapses; the same holds true for the memory and disk vendors. Most PC users have no idea how to use all the disk storage that came with their computer, but that will not stop or slow technical progress. Microsoft will take advantage of all the increasing speed and capacity and use it to improve the availability and security of the products and platforms they offer. Utility computing of one form or another will make further improvements in system availability and cost of ownership and in the end make data center computing a lot simpler.

Anticipating the future and profiting from it is a hit-or-miss process rather than a precise science. Throughout this book we have shared our secrets for trying to get more hits and fewer misses as you look at what is about to happen, not as an exercise in creative thinking but so that you can use that perspective to make decisions and pick easier paths to profit. We have quoted Wayne Gretzky, "skate to where the puck is going to be," a number of times. There is a second and less well-known quote that is attributed to him: "You miss 100 percent of the shots you don't take." We hope this book helps make your shots more accurate. Happy shooting!

Recommended Readings

BOOKS

Christensen, Clayton M. *The Innovator's Dilemma: When New Technologies Cause Great Firms to Fail.* Boston: Harvard Business School Press, 1997; paperback, New York: HarperBusiness, 2003.

Collins, Jim. *Good to Great: Why Some Companies Make the Leap...and Others Don't.* New York: HarperBusiness, 2001; paperback, 2002.

Downes, Larry, and Chunka Mui. *Unleashing the Killer App: Digital Strategies for Market Dominance.* Boston: Harvard Business School Press, 1998; paperback, 2000.

Kawaski, Guy. *The Art of the Start: The Time-Tested, Battle-Hardened Guide for Anyone Starting Anything.* New York: Portfolio, 2004.

Mason, Heidi and Tim Rohner. *The Venture Imperative: A New Model for Corporate Innovation.* Boston: Harvard Business School Press, 2002.

ARTICLES

Freeman, Kenneth, et al., "How CEOs Manage Growth Agendas," Harvard Business Review (July 1, 2004).

"The Information Technology 100," BusinessWeek http://www.businessweek.com/ (June 2004).

"The Innovation Economy," BusinessWeek (October 11, 2004).

"State of the CIO," http://www.cio.com/ (October 1, 2004).

"What Drives America's Great Innovators?" Fortune (October 2004).

WEB SITES

CIO Magazine. http://www.cio.com. News for information executives.

ClickZ Stats. http://www.clickz.com/stats/. Various Internet/online statistics.

Dialog. http://www.dialog.com. Subscription-based search tools with access to thousands of business and technical publications.

Factiva. http://www.factiva.com/. Business Information.

Fortune Magazine. http://www.fortune.com. News and information about mainstream business.

Hoover's Online. http://www.hoovers.com/. Public and private company and industry information.

IETF (Internet Engineering Task Force). http://www.ietf.org. Internet architecture and standards body.

Information Week. http://www.informationweek.com. News and information covering the IT business.

InfoTech Trends. http://www.infotechtrends.com/. Market data on computers, peripherals, software, storage, Internet, and communications equipment.

Lexis/Nexis. http://www.nexis.com/. Subscription-based search tools with access to thousands of business and technical publications.

NetworkWorldFusion. http://www.nwfusion.com/. Networking industry news.

Statistical Abstract of the United States. http://www.census.gov/pro/www/statistical-abstract-us.html. U.S. Census Bureau demographic and industry statistics.

Trade Show Resource. http://www.tsnn.com. Trade show and exhibition search tool.

VentureWire. http://www.venturewire.com/. News and information about private companies and the venture capital companies that finance them.

Washington Technology. http://www.washingtontechnology.com/. Government information technology information.

Yahoo! Finance. http://finance.yahoo.com/. Public company and industry information.

Index

About the Authors

Widely known and respected in Silicon Valley and beyond for their in-depth knowledge of the high-tech industry and the Internet's business applications, Peter Christy and John Katsaros have distinguished themselves during the last ten years as independent research analysts and consultants. Following successful careers working for some of high-tech's most innovative companies—Peter on the technical side and John in marketing and sales—they began advising technology companies across the United States. In 1994, John founded and was president of what became the largest boutique research company in Silicon Valley—the Internet Research Group (IRG)—until its sale to Jupiter Research in 2000. Peter joined IRG in 1997 as the company expanded its research offerings. In 2001, John and Peter started another boutique research firm, NetsEdge Research Group (NRG), to continue their focus on infrastructure and security innovation, covering the technology business sectors that produce the software and hardware underpinnings that all businesses use to build and secure their information technology solutions. After the IRG partners obtained the rights to use their former brand name, NRG changed its name to the Internet Research Group. Because of their demonstrated success in these efforts, Peter and John have become recognized experts and are frequently called by both the trade press and financial press for their expert opinions and invited to speak at industry conferences and company meetings around the world. IRG produces a weekly news-letter, *Internet Acceleration*, which provides an insider's view into the business and technology of IT infrastructure. To reach John and Peter via e-mail:jkatsaros@irg-intl.com and pchristy@irg-intl.com. For a free subscription to the newsletter: www.internetacceleration.com. Visit the firm's Web site at www.irg-intl.com.

John Katsaros is a principal at Silicon Valley-based Internet Research Group (IRG), a leading market research and consulting company focused exclusively on helping innovative companies gain market share. In March 2000, the original company named IRG, which Katsaros had founded, was acquired by Jupiter Communications. IRG provided strategic consulting for dozens of high tech companies, including IBM, Lotus, Cisco, Oracle, Sun, and Hewlett Packard, as well as some of the Valley's brightest venture-backed start-ups. Subsequent to working with Jupiter, Katsaros, along with Peter Christy, started a successor research company, NetsEdge Research Group which they later renamed Internet Research Group after the original IRG partners obtained the rights to use their former brand name.

Katsaros has more than thirty years' experience in senior-level sales, marketing, product development, and business planning positions in a variety of environments ranging from Fortune 500 companies to start-ups. He is also the author of *Selling High Tech* (1994), and was a contributing author to *Tricks of the Internet Gurus* (1993). He is a frequent speaker at conferences and has written many reports on electronic commerce and infrastructure. Industry and national media call Katsaros for commentary about innovation-related events. He has also appeared as an industry expert on CNBC and CNN.

Peter Christy joined IRG in 1997. After Jupiter acquired IRG he was responsible for research operations and other Internet infrastructure technologies. He was the principal analyst for content distribution, caching, and traffic-management technologies, and often provides his expertise in emerging Internet markets including Internet software infrastructure, networking and security.

Christy has been quoted in the *Wall Street Journal* and the *New York Times*, and is interviewed on Wall Street Radio, and many interactive Web publications.

Before joining IRG, Peter was president of MicroDesign Resources— a Ziff-Davis subsidiary best known for the publication of the Microprocessor Report and for convening The Microprocessor Forum. There, he was responsible for all aspects of business operations and strategy. He was also a founder and vice president of software engineering and strategic business development at MasPar Computer, a start-up focused on the design, manufacture, and marketing of massively parallel computers.

Christy has also held a broad range of technical and business management positions at leading computer companies, including Apple, Digital Equipment, IBM (ROLM), and Sun Microsystems.